Chris Packham's
BIRDWATCHING
GUIDE   FROM BEGINNER TO BIRDER

Chris Packham's
BIRDWATCHING
GUIDE   FROM BEGINNER TO BIRDER

Contents

Penguin
Random
House

Managing editor Angeles Gavira
Managing art editor Michael Duffy
Jacket designer Stephanie Cheng Hui Tan
Jacket design development manager
Sophia MTT
Senior picture researcher Sumedha Chopra
Senior production editor Andy Hilliard
Senior production controller Meskerem Berhane
Art director Karen Self
Associate publishing director Liz Wheeler
Publishing director Jonathan Metcalf

Produced for DK by
Editorial Stephanie Farrow
Design Ali Scrivens
Illustrations Phil Gamble, Ali Scrivens
Writer Rob Hume

First published in Great Britain in 2024 by
Dorling Kindersley Limited
DK, One Embassy Gardens, 8 Viaduct Gardens,
London, SW11 7BW

The authorized representative in the EEA is
Dorling Kindersley Verlag GmbH.
Arnulfstr. 124, 80636 Munich, Germany

Copyright © 2024 Dorling Kindersley Limited
Text copyright © Chris Packham (pp.6–9, 40–41,
86–87, 96–97)
A Penguin Random House Company
10 9 8 7 6 5 4 3 2
002–336924–Mar/2024

A CIP catalogue record for this book
is available from the British Library.
ISBN: 978-0-2416-3490-5

Printed and bound in Slovakia

www.dk.com

MIX
Paper | Supporting
responsible forestry
FSC™ C018179
www.fsc.org

This book was made with Forest
Stewardship Council™ certified
paper – one small step in DK's
commitment to a sustainable future.
For more information go to
www.dk.com/our-green-pledge

Introduction

Sometimes it's just a glimpse that makes the heart
flutter – that flash of blue, flick of wings, twist of tail, or
diamond twinkle of light that sparks from a hidden eye.

Sometimes it's as exciting to *nearly* see a bird as it is to meet one face to face:
to pick up a feather and know that some shy species shares your space; to hear
a fragment of song or cry that leaves you wondering what or where or why.
And there are indeed birds that will keep you waiting a lifetime for an audience,
no matter how many times you enter their court of woods or wayside.

We can be so distracted by the glamour of a rare avian superstar that
we neglect the beauty of the everyday gems on our fence or feeder. Let's
not forget the liquid rapture of a blackbird's evening melody, the gleaming
splendour of a starling's wing, or the quiet comfort of a pigeon's gentle cooing.
And of course it's not just how birds look or sound, it's what they can do that
also fuels our fascination. The science of birds can be truly sensational – how
they migrate, mark their eggs with colour, or remember where they hid their
food. There is always more to learn!

For me, the best things in life are birds, and the mission of this book is to
offer you the chance to feel the same way. Wherever we live, we can encounter
birds every day – but while we see them, many of us don't take the time to *look*,
and while we hear them, we might not *listen*. What a wasted opportunity to
experience all that wonderful life! All we have to do is stop and engage. You
don't have to be an expert, you don't need posh binoculars, and you don't
need to live on a nature reserve. All you need is a quiet moment,
some curiosity, and perhaps a mobile phone to help with
identification. Your reward may be just a fleeting smile
or it may become a lifetime's passion – either will be
free. No ticket required, no queue, and no qualifications
needed. So please read on – a life in the presence of
birds offers a whole world of simple joy.

Fieldcraft and equipment

There cannot be a human on Earth who hasn't seen a bird, but seeing is only part of the story – learn how to really look at birds and watch their behaviour, then you'll fall completely in love with them.

Free for all
A universal, accessible pastime that can be done right on your doorstep, birdwatching requires little or no outlay – just a bit of patience.

What you need

The only investment you need for birdwatching is a little bit of time. Any other skills or equipment you acquire will enhance your experience, but the most important thing is patience.

Getting started

This chapter will outline a few simple skills that can help you make the most of your time birdwatching, and talk you through some of the first steps you can take towards buying equipment that will enhance your experience. Don't be put off by thinking you need expensive binoculars, cameras, or camouflage clothing. In many cases it's not about what you've got but how you use it, and often there are very simple and relatively cheap ways in which you can modify something you might already have, such as a smartphone, to boost it into a birding aid. But if you do decide to invest, there's guidance to help you understand the options and make informed choices.

Gateway to a fascinating world

Just as you don't need lots of kit, you also don't need to invest huge amounts of time or travel to learn the skills. Birds are probably all around you, wherever you live, as they can make their home in all manner of habitats. There are simple techniques you can practise in your garden or park so that, if you then want to head off exploring the local nature reserves or further afield, you'll be ready to make the most of your trip. And when you get there, our tips will help you navigate the new territory and step further into the wonderful world of birding. The more you learn, the more you see; and the more you see, the more you'll want to learn.

Install bird feeders so you can practise your bird identification skills

Getting close to birds
As well as going to the birds, you can also encourage them to come to you.

What to wear

The good news is that there are no rules and no specialist clothing required, so just wear clothing appropriate to the conditions. It's more important to be quiet than it is to wear camouflage.

You can't hide from birds

Birds have acute vision and will notice you before you see them, so moving quietly and unobtrusively is more useful than wearing specialist clothing to blend into the background. Bright colours won't scare birds off, but loud noises and unpredictability will. Noisy, rustling clothes are not ideal, as they can give you away. While military-style camouflage is unnecessary, it is worth avoiding colours that stand out from your surroundings if you're trying to get close in order to take photographs.

It's more important to be practical and pragmatic than to kit yourself up with specialist gear, especially if you're birdwatching as a family; children grow out of waterproof clothing quickly, so it's worth considering buying second-hand too – not just from a budget point of view but also for ethical considerations of environmental impact. And should you want to exercise maximum consumer power, check that no environmentally harmful chemicals have been used in the waterproofing of any garments you buy.

Dress for the conditions

The important thing is to be dry and comfortable, so make sure you wear clothing and footwear appropriate for the conditions and terrain. Using binoculars or a telescope in cold weather can expose your fingers to the elements, so you might want to invest in gloves that work with a touchscreen. Large pockets are invaluable; they allow you to have things conveniently to hand, such as a phone, drinks, field guide, and snacks.

A peaked cap will restrict glare

Protect your head
Wear a hat to shield your head from the sun or from the cold.

Quietly does it

You might want to favour dull, muted colours to get as close as possible to birdlife, but the most important thing is to move slowly and make as little noise as possible.

In the hide

Public hides offer shelter, good views across interesting habitats, and the chance to observe birds close-up without disturbing them. Hides are also great places to meet other birdwatchers.

Visiting a hide

Hides are fixed shelters that allow you to watch birds close-up without scaring them off. The birds will know you're there, but because there are none of the dangers they associate with unpredictability, they feel safe and will generally just go about their business. Hides often have bench seats and windows, with folding shutters and a shelf. There is usually space for 10–20 people seated, plus standing room behind them for more if the hide gets busy. Hanging out in a hide is a great way to learn to birdwatch, both for practising your observation skills and developing identification techniques.

Hide etiquette

In a hide you may be surrounded by like-minded enthusiasts from whom you can learn a great deal, so engage with the generosity of that community. There may be a noticeboard listing recent sightings to watch out for, for example, and regular visitors may be happy to share their local knowledge, but do be mindful of and

Hide and seek
Sit in a hide and the birdlife will often completely ignore you, enabling you to study them close-up.

respect others within the hide who might be trying hard to listen to the birds outside.

If several people have tripods, things can get awkward, thanks to the high numbers of legs and feet – both of equipment and of people. If you're using a tripod in a hide that gets busy, it might be a good idea to take your scope or camera off the tripod and rest it on the sill, using a small clamp or beanbag to hold it still (*see pp. 26–27*). And if you see something interesting through your lens, offer to share your equipment so others can see it too, making sure that everyone gets at least a quick look, in case the bird flies away.

Don't be afraid to ask questions, either – after all, you're among fellow bird-lovers!

> *A hide isn't really somewhere to hide from birds; it just means they know where you are*

Wheelchair-users can get close to windows thanks to recesses under the sills

Full access
Many hides have gently sloping ramps for wheelchair access, and lower windows or sills.

Types of binoculars

Binoculars magnify what you see, and get you closer to the action. With such a wide selection available, it's worth taking the time to make sure you find the right type for you, so ideally try before you buy.

Exploring the options

Binoculars range from tiny compact models to heavy ones with powerful magnification. Many have rubber or waterproof casings for protection. Lenses are usually coated to help reduce reflected light and give a clearer image.

Because the objective lenses of binoculars invert the image being viewed, they contain prisms to turn the image back the right way up. There are two arrangements of prisms: modern roof-prism designs, which can be expensive but are relatively lightweight and robust, with internal focusing controls that help protect them from the elements; and the traditional porro-prism option, which can be good value, but is usually bulkier, heavier, and more fragile.

Try them out to find which ones fit your budget and needs; you need to balance ease of use and magnification against weight and price. Think about buying second-hand too, which can make your budget stretch further. And if buying new, do a bit of research if for ethical reasons you want to avoid manufacturers that support trophy-hunting.

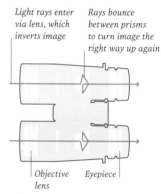

Light rays enter via lens, which inverts image   *Rays bounce between prisms to turn image the right way up again*

Objective lens   *Eyepiece*

Roof-prism binoculars
Comparatively light and easy to use, with a narrow, smooth shape.

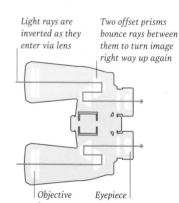

Light rays are inverted as they enter via lens   *Two offset prisms bounce rays between them to turn image right way up again*

Objective lens   *Eyepiece*

Porro-prism binoculars
As the objective lenses are wider apart than the eyepieces, the binoculars have a "stepped" shape.

Check out second-hand options to help both your budget and the planet

Ready for a close-up
Binoculars must be light
enough, easy to use, and
work well – especially if
you want a young child
to enjoy birdwatching.

Choosing binoculars

Once you've decided which design you find easiest to use, you then need to find the perfect compromise between magnification, brightness, and price. The best are expensive, but there are many good, relatively cheap (or second-hand) options on the market.

What do the numbers mean?

Binoculars are described by two numbers, such as "8x30" or "10x50". The first number refers to the magnification: i.e. 8 times or 10 times actual size. For birdwatching, anything between 7 and 12 can be useful, with 8 or 10 probably best. The second number relates to the diameter (in millimetres) of the larger (objective) lenses.

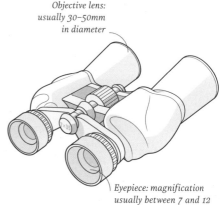

Objective lens: usually 30–50mm in diameter

Eyepiece: magnification usually between 7 and 12

Comparative brightness

Larger objective lenses let in more light to give a brighter image. So 7x50 will give a brighter image than 7x30. But 7x50 will be brighter than 10x50, as the brightness of an image depends on the size of the "exit pupil", the light entering the eyepieces. The higher the exit pupil number, the brighter the image. To work out the exit pupil size, divide the lens diameter by the magnification of the eyepiece.

$$\frac{50}{7} = 7.1\text{mm}$$

However, the quality of modern prisms, lenses, and coatings can enhance exit pupil calculations, and the best binoculars are superbly bright and clear with a very sharp image, even with a small exit pupil size, so you need to try and compare.

An exit pupil size of 7.1mm (7x50) will let in plenty of light, to give a bright image

With an exit pupil size of 5mm (10x50), less light is gathered, so the image is duller

Size versus brightness

In many situations brightness is not a major consideration, but in dull weather, on winter afternoons, or deep inside a dark wood, a brighter image is invaluable.

Relative magnification

You ideally want a close view, of course, but be aware: the higher the magnification, the more difficult it is to get a steady image, as you may experience "hand shake", although some models offer stabilization sensors. A higher magnification also gives a smaller field of view; you see a narrow area rather than a broader view – great if you are looking hard at one bird, but a wider view makes it easier to find the bird in the first place. For general birdwatching anything up to a magnification of 10 is fine.

At high magnification you get great detail, but need a tripod or other support to hold binoculars steady

x20

Some designs have image stabilization to reduce shaking even at higher magnifications

x10

At low magnification you get a wide view of the scene, but less detail, such as the number of lines on the puffin's beak

x7

This magnification is clear and bright, and you can see some of the detail of the bill pattern

Using binoculars

Binoculars are easy to set up and use, but it's worth taking a bit of time to practise and familiarize yourself with the moving parts. Follow the simple steps below to get the best out of them.

What does what

Binocular barrels pivot in the middle so you can get the right angle and width for your eyes. Many people have one eye sharper than the other, "weaker" one. If you do, you need to "balance" any difference with binoculars, just as you would if you wear spectacles. To do this, there is an eyepiece adjuster on one barrel, which you set up once (but do check regularly that it hasn't moved).

Then there is a larger central focusing wheel, which you will need to adjust constantly. The main focus is set according to distance, so you'll need to move the focusing wheel every time you fix on a new object.

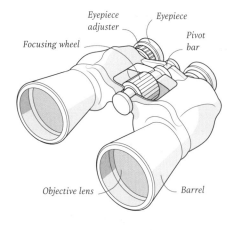

Eyepiece adjuster *Eyepiece* *Pivot bar*
Focusing wheel
Objective lens *Barrel*

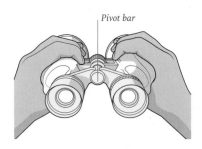

Pivot bar

1. First, set the distance between the eyepieces. This distance needs to match the gap between your eyes. To adjust, just widen or squeeze the two barrels on either side of the pivot bar.

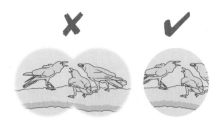

2. Adjust the width until you see a single, sharp-edged circle. No matter what films and television programmes may show, you should never see a "figure of eight".

Adjusting for spectacles

Most binoculars have eyecups that can be raised or pushed down, but many people simply raise their spectacles up and don't use the eyecups. To use them, push the eyecups down and press the eyepieces against your glasses. The field of view will be almost the same, but a bit of light may intrude from the side (you can cup your hands around the eyepieces to block it out).

Eyecup flipped up

Eyecup flipped down

What suits you?
If you wear glasses, experiment with different ways of using your binoculars to see what feels most natural.

Keep your eyes relaxed – use the focusing wheel to get things in focus rather than straining your eyes

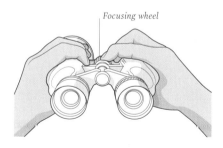

Focusing wheel

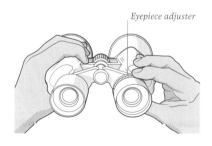

Eyepiece adjuster

3. Use the central focusing wheel to bring the subject sharply into focus. Relax your eyes, and focus on something sharp-edged, such as a television aerial or fence post.

4. Next, cover the left lens, keep both eyes open and adjust the right eyepiece. Turn it right out of focus, then slowly bring it back until the aerial or post is sharp. Note the setting and keep it there.

Fieldcraft with binoculars

The more you practise using binoculars, even just in the garden, the more you'll become familiar with them. Soon using binoculars will become second nature, like blinking or walking.

Practice makes perfect

Follow the steps below to practise your fieldcraft, first focusing on a distant object, then on birds too. A garden or balcony bird feeder is an ideal practice zone, and you'll quickly learn to "hit the target" without needing to look at the binoculars or move your head.

Keep your binoculars in a case when not in use, but leave the case behind when you are out with them. Do strap them around your neck, however – you don't want to drop them. When using binoculars, it's a good idea to shorten the strap so that they hang high on your chest, closer to your face; when you're walking along with them not in use, lengthen the strap again and put one arm through so you can tuck them under your arm for protection and stop them flapping around. Use a cover to shield the eyepieces, and look after the lenses: if you have to clean them, just use a soft cloth, very gently; dirt around the edges can be cleaned with a fingernail pressed through the cloth.

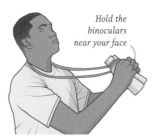

Hold the binoculars near your face

Keep your head still as you lift them up

1. With binoculars poised, scan a location with the naked eye. Have the strap short, so that when you're not holding them they hang high on your chest rather than down on your tummy.

2. When you see a bird, keep your eyes on it as you raise the binoculars to your face. Without moving your head or eyes, use your fingers to adjust the focusing wheel so the bird is in focus.

Still and steady

Hold binoculars firmly, with the thumbs underneath, and let the weight settle into your hands. To avoid "hand shake", brace a finger against forehead or chin, and to block out unwanted light from the side, wrap your hands around the eyepieces.

Choosing a scope

Sometimes, if birds are far off, you might want to go beyond binoculars for higher magnification. Choosing a scope requires a similar approach to choosing binoculars: try to find the sweet spot that works for you between magnification, brightness, and price.

Why use a scope?

Much the same applies to telescopes as to binoculars (*see pp. 18–19*). The objective lens size can vary, and magnification may be fixed, or you can have a zoom lens that gives a range. If you want to travel light, you can just use a pocket-sized scope, but it won't be as powerful as a bigger lens. The bigger the lens, however, and the more light it lets in, the larger and heavier the scope has to be. The higher the magnification, the smaller the field of view and the more it becomes vital to avoid shake by using a tripod or other support. Again, as with binoculars, buying second-hand can be a good option.

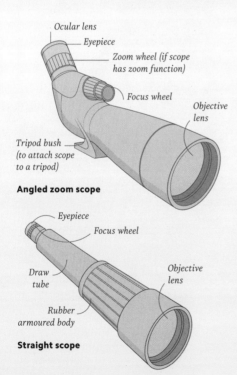

Ocular lens

Eyepiece

Zoom wheel (if scope has zoom function)

Focus wheel

Objective lens

Tripod bush (to attach scope to a tripod)

Angled zoom scope

Eyepiece

Focus wheel

Draw tube

Objective lens

Rubber armoured body

Straight scope

Which is right for you?

A fixed 20x or 30x is a good option, or a zoom, such as 15–30x or 20–60x. Magnification affects the clarity of the image, so try out different strengths and zoom eyepieces before you buy.

There are two types of scope: straight and angled. A straight scope is easy to use – you just line it up directly with the bird. You may need a bit more practice before you can easily line up an angled scope on a bird, but if you're trying to watch a bird high in the sky, for example, you'll soon appreciate the advantages of an angled eyepiece. Looking down into it may seem difficult at first, but it's really much more comfortable, especially for your neck. It's also a more practical option when sharing a scope with others, such as the taller and shorter members of a family.

Pocket power
A compact scope that fits into your pocket can give you a good view without having to carry lots of gear.

Choosing a tripod
Factor the cost of a good tripod into your budget; a pan-and-tilt one with a single handle is ideal.

An angled scope is great for sharing sightings with people of different heights

How to use a scope

How quickly you get used to your scope depends on which one you've chosen: angled scopes require a little practice at first to find a bird, and higher magnifications need support to avoid shake.

Using your scope

There's no eyepiece wheel, just a focus wheel to adjust for distance, which you can learn to fine-tune as you watch. Always keep your eye in line with the eyepiece or the image will not be clear. If you can, try to alternate both eyes; after using one eye for several minutes, you may find it doesn't focus properly for a while. You can also avoid strain by keeping both eyes open as you look through the scope, learning to "ignore" what the naked eye

is seeing. Most importantly, don't be a "scope hog" – if you see an interesting bird, let everyone have a quick look, then another longer look if there's time before the bird flies away.

Supporting your scope

There are several options for keeping your scope steady (*see below*). To stabilize yourself against the scope, rest one hand on the eyepiece, with one finger on the focus wheel and another braced against your forehead or nose. Ideally, arrange the three legs of your tripod so that two are positioned forwards and one backwards, between your legs.

Twist-and-lock
Many tripods have a simple twist-and-lock mechanism to attach a scope via a fitting called a tripod bush.

A stable platform for your scope
Simple options include using a tripod; balancing the scope on a beanbag, or fixing it to a clamp with a tripod head.

Rest the scope on a beanbag

Use a clamp fixed to a sill, fence, or car window

Adjust a tripod to suit the viewing angle and terrain

Tripod skills
Learn to adjust the tilt-control lever of your tripod without taking your eye away from the eyepiece, to follow the action and pan more easily across a landscape.

Choosing photography equipment

Taking a photo of a bird for identification and recording purposes is very different from capturing a professional-looking photograph – but it's a lot cheaper and easier too!

First steps

This is not a detailed guide on how to use an expensive camera with a huge telephoto lens; we're focusing here on practical, convenient ways to capture a good image of the birds you see, where possible just using equipment you probably have in your pocket – with perhaps just a few clever extras.

Using a smartphone, for example, allows you to share your photos instantly, and they can also be tagged, dated, and geolocated

Always ready
With a smartphone, you can quickly capture and share a shot whenever an opportunity arises.

Improvised zoom
Hold your phone against a binocular eyepiece to take a close-up photo through the lens.

instantaneously. With a few extra bolt-ons, too, you can turn your smartphone into a zoom camera: a clip-on telephoto lens can get you much closer to the action, for example, or you can put your phone into an adapter that allows you to take photos directly through a scope (known as "digiscoping"). The higher a scope's magnification, the more using a tripod for stability will help avoid "hand shake".

Taking it further

If you want to invest further, a so-called "bridge camera" is a good place to start. These can be relatively cheap and lightweight, and often the sensors capture so much detail in the image that, as well as using its zoom lens, you can crop into the image for an even better close-up too.

Another option, if your interest in photographing birds continues to grow, is to consider paying for a day's rental of a hide that comes supplied with camera equipment and is set up with tailor-made perches that are guaranteed to attract spedific birds. In that way, you can try before you buy.

There are so many clever ways to adapt technology you probably already have to take great bird photos

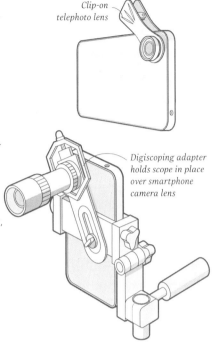

Clip-on telephoto lens

Digiscoping adapter holds scope in place over smartphone camera lens

Using a smartphone
Clip-on attachments, holders, and apps allow you to give your smartphone a zoom lens.

A built-in zoom lens is practical and convenient

Using a bridge camera
A bridge camera often has a fairly powerful zoom lens and can be controlled manually or automatically.

Photographing birds

Even with simple-to-use equipment, you'll need a bit of practice to make sure you're getting your birds centre stage. And where better to start than your own balcony or garden...?

A home hide

Set up a bird feeder outside a window of your home to turn it into a makeshift hide, and practise taking photos of the birds that visit you. Tailor the food you put out to bring a variety of birds to the feeder. Or visit a local park or nature reserve if you don't have a garden (many nature reserves have hides set up with feeders nearby).

Practising locally helps you become familiar with how to use the controls and attachments to capture the bird in frame nicely. And if you're using a smartphone, remember that the volume-down control on your headphones can be used as a remote shutter release to avoid tapping the phone screen to take a shot.

To take it to the next level, you can "stage-manage" your set-up, so that the feeder is placed in a particular setting, or against a particular backdrop, that will give you a superb photograph of your visitors. Not only will you be familiarizing yourself with your camera set-up, but you'll also become better at anticipating bird behaviour. If you have a setting for shallow depth of field, use that to blur out the background. Here and overleaf are a couple of examples I set up myself.

In a "glade"

To entice this great spotted woodpecker to my home hide, I created a fake woodland of birches smeared with fat and seeds.

1. Create a woodland by hanging silver birch logs in front of a plain backdrop.

2. Add food – which in this case was seeds stuck onto the logs with fat. Make sure the food is not visible for your camera angle.

3. Wait for your visitor
and when it arrives, take
your photographs.

On a moss post

I stood a moss-covered post in a pot, put it outside a window with seeds scattered on it, and waited for birds to visit. A nearby feeder ensured birds were already regular visitors to the area.

1. Set the "stage" outside a window so you can watch from inside, possibly through drawn curtains.

2. Position the post in front of a simple green backdrop, and adjust the angle as necessary to fill the screen of your shot.

3. Sprinkle seeds on the post and wait for a bird to arrive, such as this great tit.

Next steps

As you become more proficient, you may want to start experimenting with composition, trying close-up details for example, or action shots of birds in flight. Most bird photos look better if the eye is in focus, so for a "professional" touch when taking close-ups focus on the eye, or at least the head. It can be hard to get everything sharp in a "head-on" shot, as the head and tail may be a long way apart and the depth of focus much smaller; to get the bird more completely in focus, a side view is best – but that may be the least attractive or creative view.

In close-ups, try to get the bird's eye in focus

If your camera allows you to set a shallow depth of field, you can have sharp focus in one area and soft blur elsewhere

An action shot of outstretched wings shows a bird's structure and markings

Be organized

Get into the habit of backing up the photos you want to keep – and deleting the ones you don't (the environment is already paying the price for huge databanks of all the images we're taking, so don't keep photos you don't want).

You can use cloud storage, but it's worth also keeping a separate back-up hard drive. Keep photos organized too, with geolocation and other tags so that you can search on key words, places, dates, and bird species, or a system of folders so you can find things.

Using digital tools

It's not cheating to let the internet help you learn birding. There are some fantastic apps out there that can help you identify birds and their calls, and connect with the wider birding world.

Websites and eguides

The internet is a wonderful teaching aid. It opens up a multitude of opportunities and gives you comprehensive information at your fingertips. There are myriad websites that can offer assistance in identifying a bird, and should you want to travel light rather than carry an identification guide, you can simply download an eguide onto a smartphone. Your eguide may also have links to video and audio, to help confirm that a bird is what you think it is.

Apps and other etools

Sophisticated smartphone apps can help you identify a bird from just a picture, or pick up its song and identify it from that for you. Attachments can enhance your phone's audio capacity, too. The apps are amazing – but they're not infallible. You need to sense-check what an app is telling you if actually it's suggesting something completely inappropriate for the season, habitat, or location. Often, you'll hear a bird before you see it, but even if an app has told you what you can hear, look for a sighting too to help the information "stick"; you won't actually learn how to identify birds independently unless you look and listen for yourself. What might you expect to see? Can you hear anything familiar? Test yourself and then confirm your sightings/soundings with the apps, rather than just relying on them – that way you'll learn much more.

Be careful to choose websites, apps, and eguides that are appropriate for your geographical location, and don't just blithely rely on the internet. After all, you may not always have access to a reliable signal connection, or you may run out of battery (although it's always a good rule to carry a spare power pack to help on that score).

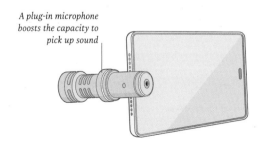

A plug-in microphone boosts the capacity to pick up sound

Audio accessories
You can fit a compact directional microphone to your smartphone, and you may also want to use a furry windshield to reduce noise.

At your fingertips
Look at websites, eguides, and your own photos to study the details of a bird: the shape of the head and beak; the colour of its legs; and details of the plumage.

Keeping notes

Using your phone to track your sightings and soundings as you go allows you to keep a log of what you find. You can set your phone up to geo-tag and date all photos and keep a record of what you encounter. Often, there's a facility within apps and eguides for you to add your own metadata tags and notes, too – but remember to back up all your information regularly, or keep a little notebook of your birding activity to help you remember what you've seen.

When you're out birdwatching, remember to give yourself time too to just watch the birds – indulge your curiosity and wonder

A place for paper

Sometimes "analogue" can be a good option instead of, or alongside, digital. Despite all the wonders of the internet, a good field guide is still a convenient reference tool, especially if you're in a hide for the day, as it won't run out of battery power, doesn't have a screen that can be hard to read in the glare of full sun, is easy to share with others, and gives you more of an overview of birds in a habitat.

Overview and detail
A good field guide will give you a comprehensive overview of a habitat and the birds within it.

Connecting with the community

So much of what we know about bird activity, numbers, and species health is down to a wonderful community of professional and amateur birders, who pool information to add to the general knowledge. As you get more confident in your sightings, you can send in your records to add to that citizen data bank, often directly via a website or app from a smartphone. One of the important pieces of information is counting birds, which you can also use your phone to help with; either take a quick photo and count from that, or download software that will do the job for you.

Join the flock
If you want to, you can connect with a local group of birders to pool information – and collectively form part of an international citizen-science endeavour.

Building your observation skills

Learning to identify birds takes time and patience, and sometimes it might seem as though information just won't lodge in your memory. There are a few strategies that can help with that.

See as well as look

Many people look but don't really *see*, especially if they're just taking photos (similarly, they often hear but don't *listen*). So, when you take a photograph, enlarge it and study it, look at the details to familiarize yourself with them. Practise this with birds on your garden bird feeder. As a starting point, use the observation process on page 44 as a framework to help you learn to work through details such as a bird's shape, markings, and legs systematically. Ultimately, with practice, it will become second nature to observe and evaluate a bird's features.

Write it down

Some people find that writing things down can help them stay in the memory better. If you're a natural list-maker, maybe keep a notebook or spreadsheet and record your observations. Your notes will help train you to really look at a bird carefully, and because you've written them down yourself, made from your own observations, the memory of them may lodge more deeply in your brain.

Practise at home
Study the details of the birds that visit your feeder to help you develop your skills of observation.

The more you practise your observation skills, the more intuitive and second-nature they'll become

Tap into your inner artist

Before you reject the idea and insist there is no artist within you, rest assured that you don't really *need* any artistic talent for this approach – honestly. It doesn't really matter if your sketch looks nothing like the bird you are trying to draw; what matters is that you are really *looking* at the bird. You're observing all the details and relative proportions of its head and body shape, length of tail and beak, arrangement of toes, and any distinctive markings or patches of colour. The resulting sketch is not the objective: it's the process itself, as that may help you fix details of individual species in your memory.

Does the bird have a "cap" of colour on its head or neck?

Are there flashes of colour on the wings?

How long are the legs relative to the body?

Keep it basic
Annotate your sketches with the features that stand out for you, to help you learn the bird's key characteristics.

Use a notebook
Making pencil sketches of the birds you see will help you study its features.

About birds

Getting to know birds – their shapes, their sounds, their individual characteristics – requires neither expensive equipment nor even patience, simply a boundless curiosity to get under their feathers.

Put the birds first

Following the birdwatcher's code of conduct will help you avoid the risk of negatively impacting any birds you are watching, by putting their interests first at all times.

Be an ally

Always try to avoid disturbing birds. Follow the rules and laws for visiting the countryside and stay on public paths to avoid disturbing birds' habitat; you could otherwise be causing birds to use up valuable energy they need for feeding, for instance, or perhaps keeping them from their young, who are then left hungry or vulnerable to predation.

Be alert to the signals and behaviour of birds, and be careful where you walk. Is a bird making repeated alarm calls, for instance? If it's breeding time, and you're on open ground or a beach, you may be too close to the nest of a ground-nesting bird.

Being still and quiet not only avoids disturbing birds, but also means that you'll see more – you won't scare off that wader on a lake shore, or a warbler in a tree, or a finch flock in a field. In close situations, such as in woodland, you'll hear most birds before you see them, and they will hear and see you too – so if you're talking as you walk, you'll hear much less, and the birds will move away.

Keep your ears open
By a reedbed or woodland path, you're mostly likely to hear a bird's call before you see it, so keep quiet and listen.

Casual encounters
Birds in a public park are often used to human company, and less likely to be disturbed or agitated by you.

Keep your distance
In open landscape such as estuaries, watch from a safe distance to avoid disturbing birds, and keep a watch on the tides too, for your own safety.

Learning to identify birds

Follow this basic framework to help you with rapidly assessing and processing information about a bird you've seen – a process that, with practice, will become second nature.

Getting started

There's no substitute for studying a field guide to get an idea of basic groups of birds (gull, tern, lark, finch, bunting, and so on) and learning the key features of each group. But these steps offer a starting point for identifying the birds you see – and the more you become familiar with the general features and geographical spread of individual species, of course, the more you can focus on the critical details and take shortcuts.

1. Context
- Where are you geographically?
- What type of habitat are you in?

Context is key, so these questions will immediately narrow down the range of species you might be looking at.

2. Season
- What time of year is it?

Some species are only present at certain times of year, so that will whittle down your options still further.

3. Visuals
- What size is the bird?
- What sort of beak does the bird have (e.g. length, shape, size, colour)?
- What is distinctive about the wing (e.g. length, shape, markings)?
- What is distinctive about the tail (e.g. proportion, length, shape, markings)?

- Is there anything distinctive about the head pattern (e.g. stripes above or through the eye, ring around the eye, or moustache)?

See pages 46–47 for useful terminology to describe them and pages 58–59 for examples of the variations of features.

4. Behaviour
- What is the bird doing (e.g. soaring, hopping, walking)?

Some birds have specific patterns of movement or habits that can help you with identification, especially if the light isn't good and you can't see their colouring clearly.

5. Sounds
- What can you hear?

Sometimes it's the call or song that will help you narrow down which species it is and distinguish one bird from another.

Black cap angular, and ragged at rear

Long black bill with pale tip

Black cap rounded

Bill red with black tip

Black legs

Underside pure white

Short red legs

Underside pale grey

Sandwich tern

Common tern

What is important?

Learn which features are important to focus on for the kind of bird you are looking at, and the points of difference between similar birds – for example, distinctive beaks, leg colours, and head markings of terns.

Behavioural pointers

If it's looking up a tree, the bird may be a treecreeper, which climbs upwards or in a spiral. A nuthatch, meanwhile, has such a strong grip it can go in any direction, and often faces downwards.

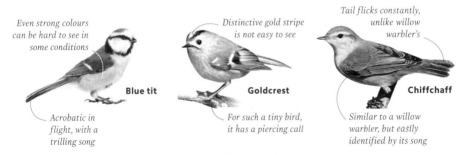

Even strong colours can be hard to see in some conditions

Distinctive gold stripe is not easy to see

Tail flicks constantly, unlike willow warbler's

Blue tit

Goldcrest

Chiffchaff

Acrobatic in flight, with a trilling song

For such a tiny bird, it has a piercing call

Similar to a willow warbler, but easily identified by its song

Putting the clues together

Colours can help you identify a bird, but against the light it can seem dark, or pale and bland, so shape, behaviour, and calls become more useful. If all you have is a silhouette, calls and song may be of help.

Anatomy of a bird

Although birds vary hugely from species to species in aspects such as plumage and size, the basic anatomy is luckily very similar, and learning the terminology will help you identify birds.

What's what on a bird

Birders use precise terminology, describing the parts of a bird very specifically to map its markings and colouration in as much detail as possible.

Understanding basic bird anatomy will also give you a huge appreciation for how brilliantly birds are built for flight: their lightweight beak instead of heavy teeth and jawbones; their lightweight yet strong skeleton; their streamlined shape and surfaces – even their legs can be tucked away to reduce drag in flight. Some birds are capable of high-speed aerobatics in short bursts, such as swallows and hobbies; others are supremely efficient endurance fliers such as godwits, which can remain airborne for days at a time, and swifts, which live on the wing for months on end.

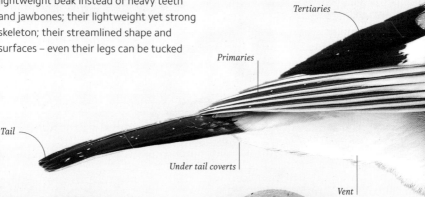

Tertiaries

Primaries

Tail

Under tail coverts

Vent

Engineered for flight

Most of the bones of a bird are hollow, to reduce body weight. Thanks to the bones' honeycomb structure, however, the skeleton is very strong. The feathers are made from the same material as human hair and nails – keratin – and different types of feather perform specific functions.

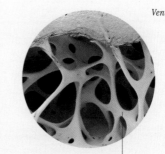

Hollow bones are honeycombed for lightness combined with rigidity

Map of a bird
Learning these terms helps you look at a bird, such as this jay, in more detail, and share information with other birders more easily.

Eye markings, such as eyebrow or eyestripe

Crown or cap

Eyering

Cheek

Nape

Scapulars

Back

Lore

Bill

Throat

Bib

Moustache

Breast

Primary coverts

Secondary coverts

Scapulars

Upper tail coverts

Secondary coverts

Primary coverts

Flank

Rump

Thigh

Belly

Leg

Toe

Tertiaries

Secondaries

Hind claw

Primaries

On the wing
Wing feathers are designed to generate thrust and lift with precise control.

A gallery of feathers

While you may not be able to get near to birds, many birds shed feathers that you can inspect close-up. The gallery opposite (not to scale) shows their beauty and variety. There are different types of feathers, each performing different functions, including sensory, insulating, and aerodynamic. The function of covert feathers, for example, is to smooth the airflow over the wings and tail; they cover the base of the different types of wing and tail feathers and are named accordingly (*see p. 47*).

Which type of feather is it?

The structure, shape, and colour of a feather will reveal not just which bird it belonged to, but where on the bird's body it came from and what its function was.

Tail feathers have a central shaft and are for steering, balance, and display

Wing feathers have a shaft off-centre and are shaped to provide power for flight

Bristles may detect prey by touch or help catch flies in the bill

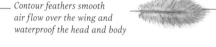

Contour feathers smooth air flow over the wing and waterproof the head and body

Semiplume feathers are weak and downy, adding insulation

Down feathers lie next to the skin and insulate a bird's body

Filoplumes are sensory feathers, but their exact function is not known

> Blue feathers are actually very rare in nature – almost all blue feathers are a result of structural colour

Untrue blue

Strange as it may seem, in nature there are almost no blue feathers: they appear blue because of the way the light is reflected from them, not due to pigmentation.

Kingfisher feather

Light bouncing off the surface of the dull, brown feather creates blues and greens

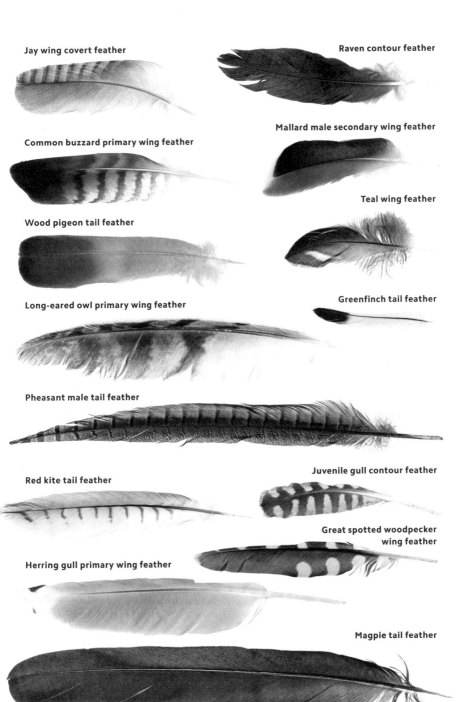

Jay wing covert feather

Raven contour feather

Common buzzard primary wing feather

Mallard male secondary wing feather

Wood pigeon tail feather

Teal wing feather

Long-eared owl primary wing feather

Greenfinch tail feather

Pheasant male tail feather

Red kite tail feather

Juvenile gull contour feather

Great spotted woodpecker
wing feather

Herring gull primary wing feather

Magpie tail feather

Colours and markings

Avian wildlife offers a wonderful variety of colour and pattern – often even within a species. A bird's plumage may be dictated by many factors, such as camouflage, breeding, and age.

Why are birds the colours they are?

Many birds are not particularly colourful (such as the "LBJs" – the "little brown jobs"), as they want to stay as inconspicuous as possible. In species where competition for mates is strong, the males are generally striking and colourful – at least during the breeding season – while females' plumage is far more restrained. In a few species this is reversed: female dotterels, for example, are bright while the males are dull. Where species have long-lasting pair bonds, such as mute swans, there is little difference between the sexes. Plumage may change as the bird matures, with the seasons, or for breeding.

Clever camouflage
Some birds, such as this juvenile wren, use colour and markings to blend with the surroundings and hide from predators. Birds such as the ptarmigan even change colouring with the seasons.

A sign of warning
The red breast of the fiercely territorial robin is not actually a cheerful flash of colour but a stark warning, to deter other robins from encroaching on its patch without resorting to fighting.

Designed to impress
While the male teal has spectacular plumage to woo a mate, the female's streaked brown plumage keeps her camouflaged on the nest.

Why birds change their appearance

Just when you think you have started to recognize some species, they change their plumage so you have yet more learning to do – but there's always a reason for those changes.

Ringing the changes

There are many reasons why birds might change their plumage: often as part of a moult, when old, faded, worn and torn feathers are replaced with new ones ready for the year ahead; sometimes as part of maturing from juvenile to adult bird; to help with seasonal camouflaging; and in preparation for courtship, when fresh, colourful plumage can help males attract a mate.

Learning all these extra variations can seem daunting. But these changes don't happen overnight, so you'll see a lot of "in-between" transitional patterns too that can help you make the connections. And, while some groups, like the gulls, go through many changes, others remain reassuringly consistent. The reward of noticing these changes, though, is an insight into what's happening in the bird's life at that moment.

Blending in
Many species have a duller plumage in winter, and ptarmigan become pure white to camouflage them against the snow.

Spring chaffinch
The male chaffinch sports its brightest, most colourful plumage in spring to attract a mate for the breeding season.

Cap, neck, and bill are vivid blue

Breast is a vibrant pink

Dull tips on new feathers conceal vibrant colours

Bill turns pink

Winter chaffinch
New feathers in autumn have pale tips that mute the blue and pink patches. The tips wear or break off in spring, so the bird changes colour without moulting.

Changing with the seasons

Although the plumage colours of some birds, such as blackbirds, are relatively constant, the adult birds of other species change their plumage with the seasons. This is to make sure that they look their best for the breeding season, before reverting to their non-breeding plumage again. For most birds, such as starlings, finches, buntings, and waders, this means dull winter colours, but much brighter hues in summer, with even the bill colour changing in many species.

For others, the pattern of change is slightly different: ducks, for instance, look their "best" in winter, when they pair up during the courtship phase, and males actually have their dullest plumage in summer. As a ground-nesting species, meanwhile, the females need no bright colours that could attract predators, so their dull plumage helps camouflage them on the nest.

All at once
Male mallards moult their wing feathers all in one go, becoming flightless for a while; during this process, the male plumage is similar to a female's – apart from the tell-tale yellow bill.

Signs of growing up

Depending on the species, a chick may goes through a sequence of moults (replacing feathers) before adopting its adult plumage. For small birds, this may take the pattern of a rapid autumn moult (usually only partial) to produce a first-winter plumage, then in spring another change into their adult plumage. For larger birds, the spring change may produce their adult plumage, or it may be only the first in a series of different plumages over a few years.

Juvenile plumage

Steps to maturity

Some large birds, such as gulls, may have second, third, even fourth-year plumages as they gradually mature into their adult plumage. As shown here, a herring gull goes through several years of plumage change.

Tan-brown with chequerboard patterning above, very dark eyes, and a dark bill

Pale pink base and tip on the bill, and greyer body feathers appearing above, but the eyes remain dark

The back shows more grey feathers

First-winter plumage

Juvenile feathers on wings and tail are faded and paler

The underparts are whiter, and the eyes are paler

Second-winter plumage

Non-breeding adult

Extensive streaking on the neck and the eyes are pale

The head is white from February to August, streaked at other times

During moult, worn, browner feathers are replaced by new black and white ones

The bill is now yellow with a red patch, and the eye is yellow

Fourth-year gulls are white below and clear grey above

Breeding adult

The underparts are a cleaner white

More grey on the back and wings

Third-winter plumage

Preening and maintenance

When they're not feeding, birds are often engaged in the essential task of preening, as feathers need to be kept in tip-top condition for flight and for weatherproofing against the elements.

Preening

Birds preen their feathers to keep them free of parasites and dirt, moisturize them with an oil they produce naturally (called preen oil) so that they stay flexible and strong, and align them in optimum position for waterproofing and flight.

In addition to preening, various other techniques are used to maintain feathers: stretching out the wings or fluffing the feathers; sunbathing; and also bathing in water, dust, or even ants (it's thought birds rub formic acid from the ants' bodies on their feathers to repel parasites).

Realigning feathers
This kingfisher is using its bill to adjust its feathers so that they are perfectly aligned for efficient flight.

Moulting

Most birds moult each year, replacing old, worn-out feathers with new, strong ones ready for winter – and for the breeding season. Juveniles moult to grow their adult plumage. Moulting takes lots of energy and can leave a bird flightless and vulnerable, so timing is key. For example, a female raptor will moult while incubating her eggs, as she is not flying then; a male will moult once the chicks have fledged and can feed themselves. Ducks are flightless when moulting in summer, before they need to migrate.

Having a dust bath
This sparrow is one of many birds that uses regular dust baths to dislodge parasites and absorb any excess preen oil they might have produced.

Bathing in water
Songbirds such as this starling will first wash off dirt and parasites before preening their feathers back into alignment.

Shaped for a purpose

In nature, form is always determined by function. Factors such as flying habits, feeding, habitat, and migration have led to myriad evolutionary adaptations – some highly specialized.

Wings and flight

A bird's flight action may be linked to its wing shape, but sometimes only loosely. Broad, bowed wings give a grey heron stability, and crescent-shaped wings help the swift dash across the sky. Warblers flit through foliage on small, round wings yet migrate across whole continents. Fingered wingtips help large birds of prey soar, while pointed wings give falcons extra speed – yet a kestrel can also hover as if suspended on a string.

Catching the wind
A gannet glides on the wind; its long wings and small flight muscles make that harder in calm air.

Soaring
Broad, fingered wings help eagles soar high up before gliding into the distance.

Life in the air
Scythe-like wings help swifts live on the wing, chasing after insect prey.

Getting around
Crows have an "all- purpose" wing shape for steady flight.

Bills and feeding

The shape of a bird's bill can be related to its feeding habits. Birds such as thrushes might have an "all-purpose" bill for eating berries, probing for worms, and catching insects. Others are more specialized: the dagger bill of the heron for snatching fish, for example, or the serrated beak of the sawbill ducks for gripping fish. Here are a few examples of the many different specialist beak shapes that have evolved.

Filter-feeding
Waterbirds such as mallards use their beaks to filter food from mud and water.

Drilling
A woodpecker's beak can chisel a nest hole in a tree and probe into bark for food.

Feet and toes

Most birds have three toes pointing forwards, and one pointing backwards, but owls and woodpeckers have the outer toe turned back for a wider grip, and some waders have no hind toe at all. Perching birds' toes are curled into a firm grip. Webbed feet push ducks and swans through water, but lobed toes do the same for coots and grebes.

Swimming
The webbed toes of this duck spread wide to push against the water on the back stroke, then fold together to slip through on the front stroke.

Climbing
Sharp claws help many birds grip bark but in woodpeckers the long third toe also points backwards, giving it extra gripping power.

Catching
Curved, razor-like claws help birds of prey catch and carry prey; an owl (shown) kills prey with its sharp claws.

Perching
A short hind toe curls around the perch, allowing perching birds such as this blue tit to grip onto a branch.

Wading
Long toes allow birds such as this egret to walk over mud and give extra support when the bird leans far forward.

Walking
Small walking birds, such as this wagtail, larks, and most pipits, have a long hind claw for stability.

Ripping flesh
Birds of prey have a hooked bill to tear flesh; falcons have a killing bite.

Cracking seeds
Finches use their wide tongue and the sharp edges of their bills to manipulate seeds.

Catching insects
Bristles and a wide base to the bill help insect-feeders such as this flycatcher snap up flies.

Probing
A curlew's long bill allows it to penetrate into silt or mud, or break up small crabs.

How bird senses work

Birds have the same five senses as us, albeit with adaptations and, in many cases, enhancements compared to our own senses. They also have other enhanced "senses", such as spatial awareness and sense of direction for navigation.

Sight and sound

A bird's eyes have more cells that capture information and carry it to the brain than we do, giving them a wider range of vision. For example, they can see colours in the ultraviolet range, which we are unable to, and the eyes of night-hunters, such as owls, are more sensitive than ours to low light. Some species have amazing visual abilities: for example, starlings can focus inside the tip of their open beak as they probe for food, while simultaneously watching the horizon for danger.

You'll often see a bird looking alert, as if watching for predators or looking for food, but usually it's actually listening. Calls and song play a vital part in birds' lives, so their hearing is excellent. In owls, the ears are located behind a disc of stiff feathers, with one ear larger or lower than the other. The minute difference in the timing of sound reaching each ear helps them pinpoint the exact position of a faint rustle in vegetation.

Wired for sound
The heart-shaped face of a barn owl acts to trap and focus sound, and a large part of its brain is dedicated to processing noises.

Touch

Some birds find their food by touch: a snipe probing the mud for worms with a bill-tip full of nerve-endings, for example, or an avocet sweeping its bill through water to "feel" for food. Sensitive bristles around the bill help insect-eating birds catch prey in flight, and flexible, bristle-like plumes let some birds detect the movement of the air as they fly.

Smell and taste

For many birds, smell and taste are not highly developed senses, although studies are revealing that they have greater significance than was once thought. Woodcocks, for example, can smell worms in the soil. Birds have relatively few taste buds, but sweet sugary tastes may make them return to valuable food such as berries.

Spatial awareness

Some birds, such as starlings and knots, form flocks that can perform highly synchronized aerial manoeuvres, but how do they not collide? How do they know when to swerve and dive? Their spatial awareness is thought to allow each bird to track just the birds around itself, filtering out the rest of the flock.

Similarly, how do birds such as swifts, swallows, and hobbies fly at speed without hitting anything? It's because their brain can filter out non-essential visual information to focus on speed and distance.

On the tip of the tongue
The sticky tip of a green woodpecker's tongue can feel and catch larvae hidden under tree bark or inside a burrow.

Starling aerobatics
Birds use optic flow – the apparent motion of static objects as we move through a landscape – to help them adjust their speed and spacing.

Identifying a bird in flight

Being able to identify a bird in flight – perhaps at a distance, or at speed, or in the sun's glare – is not easy, but learning to recognize flight actions, and wing and tail shapes, helps narrow down the options.

Distinctive flight patterns

Watch how a bird flies: some fly straight and even; others undulate up-and-down; large soaring birds save energy by soaring in circles and then gliding. You can get clues too from how a bird flocks: wood pigeon flocks tend to form long masses; rooks make busy, irregular packs; gulls often fly in lines and Vs; geese may form Vs or chevrons, although some fly in random groups. Chaffinches fly in loose groups but sparrows and linnets form tighter flocks; siskins fly in close, synchronized groups, while bullfinches do so in ones and twos. Ravens often fly in pairs, one a little behind the other. Teach yourself to take note of a bird's flight pattern, flocking habit, and wing action.

Direct
Herons and other waterfowl tend to fly in straight lines.

Undulating
Woodpeckers have deep undulations; finches, tits, and sparrows may bob and dart more, especially the blue tit.

Flap-and-glide
Birds as varied as shearwaters, swallows, pheasants, and sparrowhawks have bursts of flaps between glides.

Erratic
Owls tend to flutter and change direction, flying relatively erratically and slowly.

Soaring
Eagles, buzzards, and falcons gain height using circular soaring without wingbeats, then move off in a long, straight glide.

Shape and markings
The large size, pointed wings, and long, straight bill suggest a godwit: a white triangle on the rump and lack of white wingstripes point to a bar-tailed godwit.

A characteristic shape

In combination, the shape of the wing and the tail – and whether during flight the head and neck are long or short, withdrawn, or extended – may combine to create distinctive silhouettes in flight, both for herons, red kites, and other large birds and for smaller birds such as swifts and long-tailed tits.

Birds of prey can generally be grouped into pointed-winged species (falcons) and broad-winged birds (such as buzzards); and into those that hold their wings flat during flight and those that soar with their wings raised. Not all large soaring birds are birds of prey, however. You'll also see rooks and even cormorants circling high up too, and most large birds you see flying at a great height will probably be gulls. Tails may be pointed, rounded, shallowly or deeply forked, squared, or fan-shaped. In flight, birds use their tails as rudders for precise steering and changes of height. Many birds have similar flight patterns despite different tail shapes, however, so it is ultimately a question of watching, thinking about what you see, and learning.

At great height, or with birds flying at speed, it's hard to see markings or even overall colour, so combining overall shape and flight style and pattern will give you a good starting point to narrow down the options.

Which birds flock, and why?

Some birds are seldom seen alone, others are rarely if ever in flocks other than family groups, and some seem happy with either. It can be fascinating to watch a flock feeding – perhaps on a field or on the water – or see one performing its amazing aerial manoeuvres.

Foraging benefits

Some birds form colonies simply because good nest sites are limited, as with seabird colonies. But for other birds flocking is often to do with food: many eyes are better than one at finding food that is widely but thinly scattered. Many woodland birds stay territorial in summer, when they are nesting and food is plentiful, but flock together afterwards. Some form mixed flocks, with tits, treecreepers, and even woodpeckers coming together; the benefits can include less competition for exactly the same foods. There is much variation though: in some places goldfinches breed in colonies where food is abundant, and while species such as eiders and scoters feed in flocks, other waterfowl don't, and cormorants and shags seem happy to do either.

Protection and migration

Many eyes are also better at spotting a predator approaching, whether on the ground or up in the air, although some species, such as wrens, prefer to stay solitary, relying on camouflage and hiding away.

Entirely black, like the rook, the carrion crow is largely solitary

Although many birds migrate alone or in small groups, some species, such as swallows, will migrate in large numbers, but usually widely spread. Juveniles will often innately know in which direction to fly, but not when to stop, so some migrate in flocks with adults to learn how far to go; many don't, too – a young cuckoo, for example, migrates entirely alone. It's always worth looking at flocks in case you see an unexpected fellow traveller – migrant groups and wintering flocks can attract other birds that get "caught up" and appear in unexpected places.

If a crow is solo...
Rooks are said to feed in flocks while carrion crows feed alone – that's not quite true, but noisy flocks are usually rooks, or rooks and jackdaws.

Safety in numbers
As a peregrine falcon dives into the flock, the starlings swoop away and regroup. With so many targets for the falcon, the risk for each individual starling is minimized.

Urban high-rise
Pied wagtails may roost together to conserve body heat, even in towns and cities; small birds use a lot of energy staying warm on a cold night.

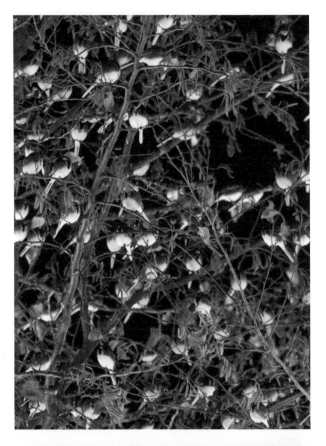

Going with the flow
Oystercatchers, like many waders, feed between high tides, when the mudflats are revealed, but then roost above the waterline at high tide.

Why birds roost

When birds sleep – alone or in flocks – they "roost". A sleeping flock
may be called a roost, as may be the place where they are sleeping.
Roosting offers security, warmth, and sometimes communication.

Warmth and safety

After a long day feeding, rearing a brood, or migrating,
roosting allows birds to recuperate and keep their plumage
in good condition. Roosting together at night (or in coastal
areas at high tide, when many birds' feeding grounds are
underwater) offers the security of multiple pairs of eyes,
so some birds flock at night even if they feed alone by day.
Roosting as a flock also lets large numbers of birds share
suitable spaces, which are often over water (such as starlings
in a reedbed), or up high (rooks in treetops, for example). For
small birds that must spend all day feeding to store energy,
roosting in groups offers shared body heat to help them save
energy and stay warm on a cold night.

Perks of age

At large roosts, such as woodland sites, older birds may get the
best places in the middle, which are warmest and least likely to
be predated. Young birds are pushed out to the colder edges,
more vulnerable to predators – and more likely to get covered
in other birds' droppings! Roosting rooks may share information
on good feeding sites, or they may simply follow the best-fed
birds the next morning.

Solitary roost
After hunting by night,
a tawny owl may roost
for the day tucked in a
tree hole or up in an
evergreen tree; white
droppings below may
give you a clue.

*At roost, rooks seem to share
information with each other on good
sites for the next day's feeding*

Giveaway calls
Hidden in the reed stems, the reed warbler may stay out of sight, but you might hear its rhythmic, repetitive, churring song.

Calls, songs, and sounds

Very often the clue to a bird's presence is not a glimpse of it but a sound. You may hear a bird long before you catch sight of it. As well as calls and songs, some birds have other, particular noises that help us track them down, too.

Not just calls

You might think birds just sing or call, but there are actually far more sounds in their repertoire, such as drumming, booming, and wing-clapping. In dense vegetation, such as reedbeds or woodland, listen carefully and you may hear birds you can't yet see, such as the tap-tap of great tits or nuthatches pecking at large nuts or seeds wedged into bark, or the quiet crack of crossbills opening pine cones, and the thud of discarded cones falling to the ground.

Pigeons do not call in flight (although the collared dove does), but pigeons and doves frequently communicate by making a loud "clap" with their wings, which is especially obvious with the wood pigeon. Their wings often whistle as they fly, too. Wild whooper and Bewick's swans make a whistling rustle with their large wings, but mute swans have a much stronger wing noise – a musical, throbbing hum that can be heard a long way off.

Headbangers

There are strange noises to be heard within a wood. All the functions of a song are replaced by a non-vocal sound when a great spotted woodpecker "drums". It rapidly vibrates its bill against a branch (or telegraph pole, if the pole makes the right noise) creating an abrupt sound that carries far through the trees.

The drumming of snipe

When a snipe dives as part of its courtship display, its outspread stiff outer tail feathers vibrate to create a "drumming" sound.

Why birds sing and call

If birdsong betrays their presence, why do some species make so much noise? How can some birds keep singing so loudly for so long? And what's the difference between a call and a song?

What are they communicating?

In general, birds sing for two reasons: to attract a mate ("listen to me, I'm clever, I'm strong"); and to defend territory ("this patch is mine, keep away"). Birds also use "contact calls" to keep in touch as they forage or in flight; these often sound similar within related groups of species. Thanks to special flaps in their throat, birds can trill and sing two notes at the same time. Some, such as the skylark, can maintain a constant output of song too. And while some birds seem to learn songs or calls in the egg, others don't pick them up until their first migration. Young birds can pick up a regional "accent" from their parents (a chaffinch in the north will sound different to one in the south, for example), and some birds even learn to mimic other birds, or other sounds (such as a phone ringtone).

Song or call?

During the day – particularly at dawn – tuneful songs are sung by many species, often by the males. Calls are shorter and more functional, such as contact calls, alarm calls, and juvenile calls for food. Hidden in his habitat, a male bird keen to mate needs to let females know, so often the denser the vegetation, the louder or more penetrating the calls (such as a bittern booming in the reeds). Warning calls are often thin and hard to pinpoint, while contact calls may be sharp or "harder" to clearly communicate a bird's position.

Ready for more
Hungry young starlings call to tell their parents that they're ready for more food.

Song in flight
As a ground-nesting bird, the skylark has no perch, so sings its beautiful song from the skies.

Sound and vision
Reinforcing his rhythmic song, a male goldcrest fans his tiny crest to reveal its orange centre.

A mighty cascade
Despite its diminutive
stature, the wren sings
loudly, frequently, and
intensely, releasing a
stream of high notes
interspersed with trills.

Learning songs and calls

Wouldn't it be wonderful to be able to recognize the calls of different birds? You can use an app as a shortcut, but there's no substitute for putting in the work to memorize them for yourself. It takes time to learn the language of birds, however, so be patient.

Listen and look

By far the best way to memorize a call is to hear a bird and then see it at the same time, so that the call sticks in your brain. It is easy to use an app on your phone, or listen to recordings on internet sites, but they won't help you memorize sound and identity together.

So, just as you should not just see but really *look*, so also you should not just hear but really *listen*. Describe the call or song in a contextual way to help fix it in your memory: the evening call of a grey partridge over the fields, the song of a skylark above the downs, or the grumpy chatter of brent geese on the estuary.

Log them down

If it helps you to remember calls and songs, write them down. Make up your own words that capture the sound for you, or use descriptive terms such as churring, trilling, buzzing, liquid, slurred, sharp, shouted; they'll help you get a grip on the "quality" of a sound. Use question marks and exclamations. Write down the pattern or form – "chwee", "chip", "chirreee" or whatever – and don't worry if you need to use a bit of artistic licence (such as the call "cu-ckoo",·which may really be nearer to "u-oo" but that doesn't quite convey the right sound).

That's not to say you shouldn't use an app – do; apps can help you isolate and connect with what you're listening to, as well as log what it is you're hearing so you can replay the call later to reinforce your learning. But if you take the time to learn the songs and calls independently, it's like being able to understand a language rather than just getting your phone to translate everything for you.

The bigger picture

Like the call of this red grouse, so many bird sounds are linked to a place, a time, a season, and these may help you to memorize them.

Getting started

Here are five relatively distinct songs that you could use for initial identification "practice". Commonly found in many parks and gardens, these birds have distinctive calls that are reasonably easy to learn. Try to watch the birds as they are singing, too, to help "fix" the song in your memory.

Great tit

Its high "see-saw-see-saw" song, often also described as "teacher, teacher", can sound a bit like a squeaky bicycle pump in action.

Robin

Clear and melodic, with warbles, whistles, and pauses, it can be described as "twiddle-oo, twiddle-eedee, twiddle-oo twiddle".

Song thrush

It varies its song, but helpfully repeats each phrase up to three times before starting the next variation, which no other common birds do.

Starling

Squawks, whines, whistles, and odd notes describe this song. It's not highly melodic, but each song can last for a minute or more at a time.

Blackbird

Its low-pitched, flute-like melodies are stronger and less melancholy than those of a robin, and without the repetitions of a song thrush.

Using an app

There are many apps that can identify birdsong with varying degrees of accuracy. Choose one that is specific to your geographical location. Make sure your phone is fully charged if you're going to rely on it to identify bird calls, and ideally carry a power pack for recharging.

A birdsong app can help you identify which birds are nearby, so you know what to look out for

Finding a mate

There are two main strategies birds use for courtship: visual display and acoustic performance. They have varied, colourful, and sometimes spectacular techniques to woo a mate.

Visual displays

The males usually do the courting, and their displays have two main functions: to impress watching females (or to reinforce existing pair bonds) and to deter rival males. In many species, males have far more colourful plumage than females, which they use to attract attention, possibly with particular sounds and actions too. Males' plumage needs to be in tip-top condition to convince females that they are the strongest suitor. The female blue tit, for example, selects a mate by the whiteness of his cheek, as this tells her

that after rearing a brood the previous year he still had energy to produce strong new feathers. Some species have specific courtship plumage, such as the tail feathers of the black grouse, the long tail of a male pheasant, and the crest of a male lapwing.

For some, courtship is a communal activity, for example the "lek" of the black grouse, which involves multiple males and females. Solitary suitors include the skylark, lapwing, and meadow pipit, who deploy a delicate song-flight to woo their mate. Often a mixture of both action and sound, courtship can be complex, such as the

Spectacular dives
To impress a female, the male lapwing tumbles and rolls in a sharp dive, its wings "humming" as it drops.

Parachute display
A male meadow pipit sings in courtship as it rises vertically, then "parachutes" down with wings half-open and tail lifted.

Shake a tail feather
In a "lek", male black grouse fan out their tail feathers, strike a pose, and make bubbling sounds to attract females.

reciprocal displays by pairs of great crested grebes, and over time pairs that mate for life can "personalize" their rituals.

Serenading with song

As part of their courtship strategy some species rely on calls, song, and other sounds, such as cooing or "clapping" their wings.

Birds such as the robin will sing from a perch, while others such as the skylark sing in flight. Some males stick strictly to a script characteristic of the species, but others might use mimicry and phrases learned from other males or even other species. In some species there are even regional "dialects" in songs and calls.

Competitive display
Male goldeneye ducks compete for the favours of a female by performing a communal display of calls and manoeuvres on the water.

Nests and nest sites

The "classic" basin of twigs in a tree is just one of a great variety of styles, shapes, and sites different birds use for their nests, from basic scrapes on the ground to intricate feats of engineering.

Builders and bodgers

Nests are not birds' homes, they are simply where they lay eggs and, often, raise their chicks. But some birds take a lot more effort than others over the building process – from the few gathered stones on a beach of the ringed plover nest to the long-tailed tit's masterpiece of lichen and feathers woven together with spider silk. And while buzzards, hawks, and kites make their own stick nests, falcons will just use old crows' nests or simply lay eggs on ledges with a bit of soft lining. Hole-nesters such as blue and great tits will use existing holes, but woodpeckers will make their own. You may easily spot the massive stick nests of rooks, ravens, and crows and the domed ones of magpies.

Location, location

Different species have their own strategies to keep their eggs safe. Many nests are up in trees or on ledges, but those made by robins and chats are hidden in banks and roots, and pied wagtails may nest in log piles. Grebe nests may float; coot nests are built up from the bottom in shallow water. Some birds nest in colonies, perhaps high in trees or out on rocky islets. If you see birds flitting around a hedge, or calling insistently, you may be close to a nest. Whatever you do, avoid disturbing them, as this may cause them to abandon the nest, or you may alert a predator to its presence.

Under the eaves
House martins build their mud nests under the eaves of buildings.

On the ground
The eggs of a ringed plover are camouflaged amid the shingle.

On a rocky ledge
A guillemot will lay its eggs on just a bare ledge.

In a tree
The soft, warm nest of
a long-tailed tit is lined
with up to 1,500 feathers,
and covered in lichen
for camouflage.

Raising a family

There are many variations on how many eggs a female lays, what colour they are, and what happens after hatching. Where the nest is placed plays a part in what occurs next, too.

Clutches and broods

A "clutch" is a batch of eggs, which hatch to become a "brood" of chicks. Eggs are laid with myriad patterns: hole-nesting species may have white eggs that they can see in the dark; others may be camouflaged (such as a robin's) or even sky-blue (a song thrush's).

Species such as seabirds may lay one or two eggs, while tits for example may lay 10 or more. Some birds only rear one brood per season, others up to three or four. Sometimes a single large brood will coincide with an abundance of food; other birds produce smaller broods over the summer with a less plentiful supply of food. Even similar species may have different strategies: tawny owls always nest in the same territory, laying few eggs, while short-eared owls go wherever the food is, laying more eggs in some years but none in others.

Ready for action – or not

Some chicks, such as those of ground-nesting species, are "precocial", meaning they hatch pretty much ready to be mobile and feed for themselves. Other chicks are "altricial", staying in the nest until they develop feathers and "fledge" (take their first flight). Vulnerable to predators and reliant on their parents for their food supply, the chicks may even become heavier than their parents as they build up energy reserves for their first flight.

Ready to fledge
Well-developed within the egg, the chicks of this mute swan hatch ready to swim and feed, although they cannot fly for 17–22 weeks.

When timing is key
Blue tits time the hatching of their brood to coincide with the emergence of the chicks' favourite food, winter moth caterpillars, and each chick may eat 100 a day.

Finding food

Foraging for food takes up a huge part of many birds' daily lives, and different species have developed their own techniques, from physical adaptations to behavioural strategies. Habitat decline and climate change add to the challenges they face.

The need to feed

Few birds can fast for long. Small ones in particular must feed constantly to stay alive, especially when preparing for a long migration, or during the cold days and long nights of winter, when keeping warm uses up a lot of energy.

While some birds flock together to maximize their chances of finding food, some species have evolved to become specialist feeders, such as the green woodpecker, which has a sticky tongue that is perfect for collecting ants' eggs, or the serrated edges of a sawbill duck's beak, which is ideal for holding onto a wriggling fish. Other birds use techniques rather than adaptations: herring gulls will drop shellfish onto rocks to break them open, for example, while song thrushes bash snails against a stone. Species such as nuthatches and jays even store food for later, while others simply steal: a great black-backed gull will mug other seabirds for their catch.

Clever strategies
The oystercatcher can hammer shells open or slide its bill between the two halves to prise them apart.

Evolved adaptations
The tweezer-like beak of a crossbill is ideal for extracting the seeds inside pine cones.

Habitat is key

Access to unpolluted habitat is vital. Grebes and herons, kingfishers and goosanders, kittiwakes and terns all need clean, healthy water for their fish prey to thrive, so pollution can spell disaster. Likewise, estuarine birds need rich foraging habitats of wet mud, washed and refreshed by unpolluted tidal waters. Pollution, sea-warming, and over-fishing all present threats to bird populations.

Farmland once gave much more food for many birds, but intensive farming practices have seen, for example, the loss of meadows on which owls and kestrels would hunt for prey; of safe nesting sites for lapwings; and of stubble fields once alive with huge mixed flocks of finches, sparrows, and buntings. Pesticide use has drastically impacted the insect food needed by swallows, larks, and so many other birds. Gulls still "follow the plough", seeking worms and other food turned up with the cultivated soil. Regenerative and other wildlife-friendly farming practices may help redress the balance in future.

Feeding as a flock
Where food is temporarily plentiful, small birds such as linnets and other finches may forage together as a mixed flock.

The importance of margins
Hedges, field margins, and "messy" areas contain the vital native plants birds need, like this thistle providing seeds for a goldfinch.

At home with hippos
Spending the summer breeding by the rivers of Europe, the common sandpiper makes its winter home among the wetlands of Africa.

Where do they go?

Bird migration has long been one of the great mysteries of the natural world: around half of northern European species migrate each year, but how do they know where and when to go?

Incredible journeys

Migration is chiefly a means of maximizing birds' exploitation of available food – but that doesn't do justice to the remarkable or even epic flights that this can sometimes involve – the navigation skills, endurance, and dangers.

Imagine yourself as an adolescent, without education, maps, signposts, books, TV, or the internet. One day you have such an irresistible urge to go that you start to head off to Africa: how do you even know there is such a place, let alone where it might be? Nevertheless, off you go, to spend a winter in Africa, before returning unaided back to your garden. You have just replicated the actions of a cuckoo, swallow, willow warbler, or whitethroat. These birds, wonderfully, return to the very same tree or the very same shed where they bred the year before, or where they were reared.

Some birds, such as ospreys, common terns, and swifts, fly off to Africa but do not return for a couple of years, when they will be old enough to breed. Waders navigate the whole of the Arctic and subarctic regions, flying huge distances from the far north to spend the winter on our estuaries. Bewick's swans and brent geese fly in from Siberia every autumn and return there in spring. Seabirds spend the winter at sea, often with an eyeline just above the waves, but return unerringly to their native cliffs and islands.

Masters of navigation

Some species fly directly, others take winding routes along landmarks; some fly out and back along the same route, others have a more circular journey; some stop and feed along the way, others tackle the whole journey in one non-stop flight. Over short distances, at least over land, landmarks can be used, but more often birds rely on detecting and interpreting magnetic fields, using magnetic material in the bill and special cells in their eyes. They may also navigate by the Sun and stars.

But how do they know which direction to go in, when, and how far to fly? Much of the information about direction and distance of flight is, incredibly, encoded in their genes, and an internal clock lets them know when it's time to migrate. They also learn from experience, so their first migration is always the most perilous.

Tell-tale clues

It's easy to develop a keen eye for giveaway signs of bird activity, even if the birds themselves are out of sight. With a bit of detective work, you can still establish which birds are active around you.

Signs of habitation

Seeing a nest is not always about looking up into a tree; it may be twigs on a ledge, for example, or holes tunnelled into a sand bank. Bird poo – on the ground or on rafters – is a sign of roosting activity.

The poo is actually the black stuff; the white is the urine (it's not very watery because birds tend to conserve water to help guard against dehydration). Similarly, you might see pellets regurgitated by birds on the ground. Pellets contain all the undigested parts of their food, such as fur, bones, scales, feathers, or even just seed husks. Many birds make pellets, but you're mostly likely to spot those made by owls and raptors, or maybe those of a kingfisher or heron.

Other signs of birds feeding might include, for example, holes drilled in a tree trunk by a woodpecker, or hazelnuts jammed into a bark crevice – a possible sign that a woodpecker or nuthatch has been trying to hammer the nuts open.

Often the clues are on the ground, so remember to look down as well as up

Dents in tree bark
Look for hollows made by treecreepers that roost in Wellingtonia tree bark.

Burrows in a bank
Sand martins make their nests in holes burrowed into a sandy bank by a shoreline.

Pellets on the ground
Owls and other birds drop regurgitated pellets, revealing traces of their latest meal.

Signs of other activity

Scattered feathers in a cavity or on the ground may be from a bird moulting nearby or, particularly if they are the fluffy inner layer of down feathers, a recent kill on a predator's plucking post. You may spot egg fragments on the ground too, but these are not always signs of a nearby nest, as parents may drop hatched eggshells away from the nest to divert attention, or the egg may have been predated. You may even be able

Ghostly sign
Glass is confusing for birds, and many fly into windows – sometimes fatally. Impacting at speed, as this pigeon did, leaves a clear imprint on the glass.

to work out whether it was taken by a predator: an egg that hatches naturally when a chick emerges usually breaks in half quite cleanly; on predated eggs, the breaks are likely to be more irregular.

Holes in trees
A woodpecker keen to feast on the insects within can whittle away at a tree trunk.

Pine cone husks
A pine cone stripped clean of its seeds betrays the activity of an efficient crossbill.

Fragments of eggshell
Bits of shell suggest a hatched chick is nearby – or, in this case, that a predator ate it.

Bringing birds
to you

Often you have to go to the birds, but sometimes you can encourage them to come to you – and when they do, you will find that there's nothing better than sharing your space with a wild creature.

Creating a bird-friendly space

There are many ways in which you can adapt your outdoor space to be as attractive as possible for birds – and even a small roof terrace or balcony can support bird activity.

Providing for their needs

Birds need food, water, a place to roost, and somewhere to nest. If you can provide any or all of these elements, then you can attract birds into your outdoor space. As well as hanging bird feeders in strategic positions, think carefully about what you choose to plant. The flowers you grow can entice insects on which birds can feed, and later in the year they may produce seeds or berries for birds to eat in autumn and winter. If

Feeding station
Blossom trees attract insects, which in turn draw birds such as these tree sparrows, relatives of the more common house sparrow.

you have space for native shrubs, and hedges rather than fences, you're offering places to nest, which you can also supplement with nest boxes.

One of the best things you can do for wildlife in your garden is to make sure there's water in it: a large pond is obviously great, but a simple bird bath or a little barrel or trough pond is fine too. Water offers a space for birds to drink and bathe, and it also attracts insects for them to feast on.

Other simple steps

Even how you garden makes a difference, so try to leave some "untidy spaces" that provide insect habitats, such as stacks of plant pots or logs, and patches of moss and spiders' webs that are useful for nesting materials. Avoid pruning during the nesting season or when plants are covered in berries, and never use pesticides or insecticides. Finally, be realistic: if you have cats in your garden, you may not get as many birds.

Windfall fruit makes a feast for blackbirds

Don't be too tidy
Leave fallen apples, seed heads, and berries for the birds to feed on in winter.

The size of the hole in a nest box will determine which species feels safe and makes it a home

Feeders and boxes

Bird feeders and nest boxes can turbo-charge the potential of your outdoor space as a supportive environment for birds, but choose them carefully and hang them wisely.

Choosing bird feeders

You have three key factors to consider: which type of feeder to get; what food to put in it; and where to hang it. Each choice you make will influence the species that visit and how attractive the feeder is to birds. Many types are designed to favour small birds, with springs to deter heavier ones, or are engineered to be squirrel-proof – sadly, not always successfully. Look at online reviews or ask other bird-lovers for recommendations.

Choose from a variety of foods: nuts, seeds, grains, and suet balls or pellets will all meet the needs of different birds. Mix and match, or make your own, and help birds by tailoring the menu for the time

of year – high-energy seed mixes in the breeding season, for example, or before migration. To avoid spreading bird flu and other diseases, it's vital to clean feeders regularly. Soak them in soapy water, then dry thoroughly before refilling. If you see a dead bird, wash out your feeders and wait a few weeks before rehanging.

Where you hang them makes a big difference; birds will not use a feeder if they don't think it's safe. Are there perches where they can stop and check for predators, or are there pets or people nearby that might scare them off? Create a feeding station if you have room, ideally somewhere where you can discreetly watch them feasting.

What's on the menu?
Different feeders are suited to particular foods. Make your own from recycled bottles, or try the latest squirrel-proof technology.

Choose suet and fat balls without mesh bags, as birds' feet can get trapped in the mesh

Hanging nest boxes

Bird habitat has declined hugely, but putting up nest boxes offers birds a ready-made home. As with feeders, different types of box will attract particular species, and where you site them is key. Whether you buy boxes or make your own, check the dimensions and design to make sure the holes are the right size for a particular species, and not too close to the floor (so chicks leap out too soon). Research instructions on positioning of nest boxes for the birds you want to support, whether up a tree, high on a wall, or on a fence – and do clean the boxes each year to avoid spreading disease.

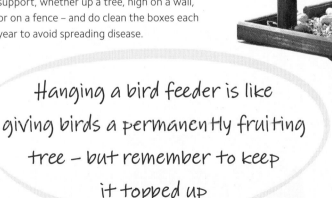

Hanging a bird feeder is like giving birds a permanently fruiting tree – but remember to keep it topped up

Hedge fund
Hedges offer shelter and nest sites for birds such as this wren. Ivy berries still provide birds with food too, after other berries are over.

Choosing your plants

The plants you grow can actively support birdlife, whether supplying food in the form of insects or seeds, materials from which to build nests, or shelter and nest sites.

Flora for fauna

You can tailor what you plant to support as wide a range of different birds as possible, or create specific conditions that are especially appealing to particular species. Plants with nectar-rich flowers will attract insects such as beetles, hoverflies, butterflies, and aphids, many of which (including their larvae or caterpillar forms) are food for insect-eating birds. Don't forget, too, that a particular flower may feed the adult insect, but their grubs or caterpillars might need other plants altogether.

Look beyond your garden to see what wild flowers and seed heads are buzzing with feeding activity, and maybe leave a little "wild patch" in your garden if you have space, or grow a mini-wildflower meadow in a windowbox. Artificial grass is an ecological disaster, and even a flawless lawn is of little use to wildlife, so let the worms and insects cohabit amongst the grass to give the starlings, robins, and blackbirds a reason to visit you.

If you have room, try to echo the way nature grows in layers, with ground cover, shrubs, and a tree canopy. Favour hedges full of native berry-producing shrubs over fences, or at least plant climbers up your fences, such as honeysuckle, which offers summer nectar and autumn berries, and ivy, which still provides food when many other plants have finished flowering. Try to grow a range of plants that will provide food throughout the year.

Insect larder
Blackbirds and others feast on the insects drawn to nectar-rich plants, and on the grubs and caterpillars they produce.

Nest-building materials
Kind gardeners leave moss, twigs, and dry grass that can all be put to good use by tits, finches, and other nesting parents.

Seeds to feed on
Leave the seed heads on plants after flowering, to provide birds such as this greenfinch with a source of food.

Providing water

A small pond with some natural, native plantings offers other creatures a home, but even a small, shallow bird bath on a roof terrace gives birds a place to drink and bathe.

Birds need water

Hydration is very important for birds, so any water feature you can offer will give them drinking water. They must also bathe regularly to keep their plumage in good condition. Some, such as house martins, need a nearby source of water to supply the wet mud from which they build their nests.

A shallow pond with natural, native plants provides a home for many creatures; it is a magnet for insects, and therefore everything that feeds on insects too, such as birds, frogs, and hedgehogs. If you don't have much room, even a shallow barrel pond, trough, or small bird bath with gently sloping edges can offer birds a place to drink and bathe.

Use rainwater from water butts if you can rather than tap water (which contains additives), and keep water levels topped up; it's unfair to get birds used to a food supply or drinking water and then forget it at a critical time. If you live in an area where the water might freeze in winter, you could put a floating ball on the water to prevent it icing over completely, but never add anything such as antifreeze. "Fake" ponds using mirrors, or any large hanging outdoor mirror too, can be lethal for birds; they may see a reflection in it (or in a window) and try to fly through it, with often fatal results.

Simple saucer
A plant saucer, topped up regularly, makes an ideal bird bath, but only put it at ground level if there are no predators nearby.

In a barrel
A barrel with a few aerating plants is small enough even for a balcony. Keep one area shallow for any creatures trying to get out.

Pond life
A shallow pond with mud patches and overhanging twigs and plants creates ideal conditions for a thriving, bird-friendly ecosystem.

Habitats

With 10,000 species in the world, birds will often surprise you by turning up in very unusual places, but thankfully they do often stick to particular habitats that you can explore.

Keep your eyes peeled
Some birds are habitat specialists, but others are opportunists and most fly over almost anywhere, so you never know what you might see.

Exploring bird habitats

This chapter outlines some of the primary habitat types and provides a simple field guide to the birds you might find within them, from parks and gardens to sweeping shores and wild moors.

Right place, right bird

Habitat requirements can be very broad or very precise. Birds that like open ground with short vegetation, such as a skylark, might find their requirements met in such varied territory as fields, airports, dunes, downs, moors, and heaths. Pied wagtails might be found anywhere from watersides and sandy beaches to footpaths and suburban car parks. As long as there is food and shelter, many birds are likely to be found in multiple habitats.

Yet the basic need for the right habitat, at least when breeding, is a good clue to the likelihood of seeing any particular species, should you be in a wetland, a woodland, on hills or downs, in farmland, or by the sea. There is a strong connection between a bird and its bush, or its reedbed or shingle spit, or peatbog or mountain plateau. For some, habitat has a very narrow definition: to find breeding bearded tits, for example, you must look in a reedbed – nowhere else will do.

Habitat as identification aid

It will become second nature to think of this connection between habitat and breed when you see a bird you can't immediately recognize. Such a close relationship can quickly narrow down the options as to what birds you might be seeing in a particular habitat, and the field guides in this chapter will help you, although do note that the birds are not to scale. However much you try and categorize a bird, though, remember that they can fly wherever they want, so habitat alone won't provide all the clues; you need to evaluate the details of a bird, and take into account the season too (see pp. 44–45).

Remember, when exploring habitats in different seasons, to make sure you dress for the terrain and the elements. Be aware of the weather forecast, tide times, and other factors appropriate for the area you're exploring. Know the rules for visiting the countryside, sticking to public-access areas and being respectful of the rights of others. And, of course, keep the birdwatcher's code in mind: always put the interests of the birds first (see pp. 42–43).

Resident birds
Small songbirds such as the robin are completely at home in many gardens, which resemble their natural bushy, woodland-edge habitat.

Gardens and balconies

Gardens, terraces, and balconies offer a variety of micro-habitats for birds, and also give you a convenient place in which you can start practising your birdwatching skills.

A little of everything

Once you start to watch out for them, you might be surprised just how many birds are sharing your outdoor space with you. From lawns full of worms and ants for pigeons, thrushes, and starlings, to flowerbeds, shrubs, hedges, and trees for robins, dunnocks, finches, sparrows, and tits, there is the potential in a garden for a great range of birdlife. Even a small balcony can support plants that produce seeds or berries, or attract insect life on which birds can feed. Hedges, shrubs, ivy-covered walls, and nest boxes also offer some birds a nest site, as do garden sheds, building eaves, and old outbuildings; in summer, house martins and even swifts may nest there, so keep an eye on the skies and you may see them feeding overhead.

Some garden birds are common visitors, while others are seasonal migrants. At sunrise in spring, the persistent singing of male songbirds to maintain their territory is known as the dawn chorus. Once families have fledged, many must move away to feed elsewhere if a garden can't support the additional numbers; birds may move away until the population adjusts, returning to the garden once there are more berries, fallen apples, or other food for them. Then, in winter, the residents are joined by a few winter visitors, while the summer visitors migrate elsewhere until the next spring.

Nests and fledglings
In spring, watch for signs of nests, such as adult blackbirds flitting repeatedly in and out of a hedge to feed their brood.

Autumn resources
Gardens can offer food when natural habitats are depleted, so visitors such as this blackcap might appear, in search of berries.

Winter refuge
If frost makes feeding difficult in open fields and the hedgerow berries have all gone, you may see visitors such as redwings.

Birds of garden spaces

The birdlife visiting your outdoor space will vary depending on where you live, on the time of year, and on the trees, bushes, and plants growing there.

White cheek between black cap and chin

GREAT TIT
12–14 cm

Small, energetic and boldly coloured, the great tit uses a wide variety of calls and strident songs and can be found from ground level to treetops.

BLUE TIT
12 cm

This popular visitor to the bird feeder is tiny, colourful, and acrobatic. It can appear more green and yellow than blue.

Blue cap and white face, with a black stripe and border

Female is brown with yellow beak; juvenile is paler, rusty-brown with dark beak

Tail is longer than the body

LONG-TAILED TIT
14 cm

With high, sharp calls, these nimble little birds swoop in small groups, playing "follow the leader" across open spaces between trees.

BLACKBIRD
23-29 cm

Often found hopping across the lawn, the blackbird has a flowing, musical song but hysterical, rattled alarm call.

Male is glossy black with yellow beak

Short dark tail with white rump and throat

SWALLOW
12–20 cm

Perched on an aerial or wire, these summer visitors are fast, fluid, and agile in flight. Listen for their slurred song, and spot their nests in shed rafters.

HOUSE MARTIN
12 cm

Look for their mud-cup nests under house eaves and spot the distinctive white rumps as they circle over rooftops in summer.

Glossy blue back and dark throat

Long forked tail with white band; pale underparts

Hang a bird feeder near to a window and your house becomes a hide

SONG THRUSH
23 cm

A common sight on a lawn or vegetable patch, this thrush sings short, strident phrases, each repeated two or three times.

DUNNOCK
14 cm

This small, dark, sharp-billed bird can be spotted shuffling through flowerbeds and shrubs.

Male has a grey crown and black bib

Female is dull olive above, buff beneath

HOUSE SPARROW
16 cm

A noisy, sociable little bird that likes dense thickets and roof tiles and gutters, it is often found around people.

Male has rusty-red underparts

♀

Female is unmarked below, with a pale stripe behind the eye

GREENFINCH
15 cm

A regular near tall hedges and on bird feeders, the greenfinch has a bat-like display flight with a ringing, chattering song.

CHAFFINCH
14–15 cm

This small bird, marked with white, is regularly found cheekily searching for scraps. Its cheerful, rattling song has a final flourish.

Glossy, with a green and purple sheen

ROBIN
12–14 cm

This small bird drops from its perch to pick food from the ground and sings a strong, melodic song.

STARLING
20–23 cm

The seemingly black feathers of this bird have an iridescent sheen. See it bathing, feeding on the lawn, or flocking in noisy, chattering groups.

Orange-red breast is brightest in autumn, fading by midsummer

Pale stripe over the eye, and barred across wings

WREN
6–10 cm

A tiny, bouncy, bobbing bird that keeps low, with agitated, churring calls and a fast, vibrant song that includes a rapid trill.

Grey body and pink breast

Black neck ring on adult

COLLARED DOVE
32 cm

Slim, pale dove often found on a lawn or TV aerial. The underside of its tail is black with a white tip and its song is a triple "cu-cooo-cuk".

WOOD PIGEON
40–45 cm

Big pigeon with a white band on its wing, white neck patch, and pale band and black tip under tail; its song is "cu-cooo coo, cu-coo, cu-cooo cuk".

Canada geese
These large geese, introduced from North America, are relatively bold and curious around their human neighbours.

Parks and park lakes

You can learn a lot about birds in the park, where they'll be relatively relaxed around people. This gives you a chance to hone your identification skills and study them closely.

Up close and personal

With people always around, park birds are mostly tame, opportunistic, and adaptable. Other than in a garden, this is commonly the easiest habitat in which to practise birdwatching and see different species.

Visit regularly through the seasons and you can study the various plumages of a species. You can compare those of a mallard, for example – juvenile, female, and the male in winter and in summer, when it looks more like a female but keeps the yellow beak. Look at the gulls, also showing a variety of plumages according to age and season, but with no difference between the sexes. Then there are coots and moorhens; although they keep the same plumage all year, the juvenile plumage is different to the adult's, so you can learn to identify the young ones.

Chaffinches and sparrows come for crumbs, while jays and woodpeckers keep their distance but are still there to be seen and heard. You'll soon learn the songs of chiffchaffs and blackcaps, and how to tell a grey wagtail from a pied wagtail. There is plenty to enjoy but also plenty of opportunity to practise your identification skills if you take the time to look and listen.

Spring chicks
In spring, look for mallards shepherding their orderly brood of ducklings out onto the water.

Cheeky chaffinch
This colourful little finch might boldly help himself to the leftover crumbs on your picnic table.

Nesting in style
At a lake see different nests, such as the coot's, on solid ground, or the floating nest of a grebe.

Birds of parks and park lakes

Visit your local park to practise identifying birds; a park lake, for example, can help you learn to distinguish common water birds that may be more abundant elsewhere, but also farther from you.

MUTE SWAN
120–170 cm

Happy by or on the water, this huge, orange-beaked swan will come near for crumbs – but gives a warning hiss if you get too close.

Black knob on orange bill

Adult bill is orange; juvenile bill is grey

White forehead and bill

COOT
36–38 cm

A medium-sized black bird with a white face and beak, usually found walking by, or swimming and diving in, open water.

Red-brown cap on female/ juvenile ♀

Black cap on male

BLACKCAP
14 cm

This small, stocky, greyish warbler is found in dense shrubbery. Listen for its "tak" call and richly musical song.

Black and bright yellow headstripes

CHIFFCHAFF
10–12 cm

You may hear it singing its name – "chiff-chaff" – before you see this small bird in trees and bushes. Most visit from March to October, although some do overwinter.

Similar to a willow warbler, but with darker legs

GOLDCREST
8–9 cm

Found in trees and bushes, this tiny bird is barred black on its wing, and has a high, simple call and rhythmic "diddle-di-dee" song.

Head to the park early in the morning, before it gets too busy, to see maximum bird activity

Head is dark brown in summer, white in winter

BLACK-HEADED GULL
45–53 cm

This relatively small gull has a white edge to its outer wing, pale grey upper parts, and a red bill and red legs.

Male bill is bright yellow; female bill is orange and brown

MALLARD
50–65 cm

A coarse "quack" helps you identify this large, orange-legged duck. Males are brightly coloured; females are streaky brown with a blue wing patch.

Black head and neck, with white chinstrap

Grey-brown back and white rear

CANADA GOOSE
75–110 cm

Often found grazing on short grass by the waterside, the black-necked Canada goose is large, with a loud honk.

Plumage seems black, but is iridescent green

STARLING
20–23 cm

Although similar to a blackbird, the starling is smaller and shorter-tailed. Listen for its rapid, varied, imitative song from rooftop or wire.

Bright red-and-yellow bill

White marking on tail and flank

COLLARED DOVE
32 cm

The neck ring gives this slender dove its name. The underside of its tail is black with a white tip, and its song is a triple "cu-cooo-cuk".

MOORHEN
30–38 cm

Rather than diving like a coot, a moorhen creeps and swims at the water's edge, and its body is grey and brown with white markings.

Black neck ring on adult

Long droopy tuft on the back of male's head

PIED WAGTAIL
18 cm

Find this pretty bird on the ground, walking along a path or car park with its classic bobbing tail. Its call is "chissik" or a musical "tschu-ee".

Male is black-and-white; female is greyer

TUFTED DUCK
40–45 cm

On the water this bird will happily drift along, although it frequently dives under to feed too. Males are black and white; females are chocolate-brown, but both have yellow eyes and blue bills.

Urban areas and waste ground

Despite the constant hum of activity in cities and towns, some birds manage to make themselves at home on patches of green space, building roofs, and even car parks – or on waste ground, which offers many more opportunities.

Finding a way to thrive

Birds are more adaptable than you might think. Kestrels and the once-rare peregrine, at home on clifftops and rocky ridges, have learned to breed on tall building ledges high over the city and feed on insects and rodents. The plentiful population of pigeons is "feral", domesticated from wild rock doves long ago, but since gone back to the wild; "pure" rock doves are now rare.

Gulls nest on flat roofs and eat scraps even in the busiest high street. The rubbish we throw away can contain a lot of food for birds. It attracts other creatures, too, which some birds can eat. Even tarmac, concrete, and roadsides can house insects on which birds can feed. Rooks pick dead flies from parked cars, and wagtails attack their reflections in wing mirrors. You might even hear the scratchy song of a black redstart – a real rarity – if it settles on a factory or railway station roof. Unused land that becomes overgrown with thistles, brambles, and other plants can host a greater variety of birdlife, especially in autumn and winter, when busy flocks of goldfinches, linnets, and house sparrows appear.

City hunters
Kestrels nest on rocky cliffs in the wild, but have adapted to nest on the high ledges of city buildings.

Street scavengers
Gulls and pigeons are very opportunistic and adaptable, finding plenty to eat amongst the food we humans discard.

Park patrol
Look down in a car park and you might see this pretty little bird, tail bobbing characteristically as it struts around.

Stop the traffic!
Although they usually nest in a tree rather than a traffic light, mistle thrushes are famously aggressive near the nest, so are not for moving.

FERAL PIGEON
29–37 cm

This fast, bold bird has varied colours and patterns. Descended from the wild rock dove, it is extremely well-adapted to urban living.

PIED WAGTAIL
18 cm

See this little bird on paths, paved areas, and patches of grass, bobbing its tail as it walks around looking for insects, seeds, and scraps of food.

Striking red and yellow markings on wings and head

May be grey, white, brown, or patchwork colours

GOLDFINCH
12–13 cm

The handsome goldfinch can often be found on overgrown wasteland, feasting on the seeds of thistles and similar "weeds".

Males have crimson on chest and forehead

LINNET
13.5 cm

This little brown finch feeds on the ground, searching for seeds. In winter, linnets will typically flock together.

SWIFT
16–17 cm

Usually flying high with a screeching call, the acrobatic swift will never be seen on a wire or ledge. It arrives in summer and nests in roof eaves.

Distinctive "boomerang" wing shape and notched tail

White streaks on wings and tail

Tail is forked, with long elegant streamers

Bluntly forked tail and white underside

SWALLOW
14.5–20 cm

You may catch this sleek, agile summer visitor swooping to catch insects on the wing, or see a row of them perched on a wire.

HOUSE MARTIN
12 cm

Smaller than a swallow or swift, this summer migrant can be found in towns if the air quality is good enough, but needs mud to build its nest under eaves.

Birds of urban areas and waste ground

On "waste" or derelict ground, patches of vegetation, and rooftops you'll find birds living and foraging. Strangely, seabirds – gulls – are some of the most successful at adapting, and they even nest on roofs, far from their coastal strongholds.

Look carefully and you may see a kestrel or swift soaring overhead, or a pied wagtail on the path

Mostly black, with a white belly and white patches

White head heavily streaked in autumn-winter

The glossy black feathers shimmer with greens and blues

LESSER BLACK-BACKED GULL
51–64 cm

Often slightly smaller than a herring gull, this bird has a darker, slate-grey back and wings, and bright yellow legs.

Pale grey back and wings

Red spot near tip of bill is common to both gulls

Wing tips are black with white spots

MAGPIE
46 cm

This member of the crow family, with its unmistakable black-and-white plumage, can often be found in urban habitats.

HERRING GULL
55–65 cm

A large gull with pink legs, the herring gull is bold on the ground and loud in the air. A native of cliffs, it has adapted to urban ledges and roofs.

Head stays completely still when it hovers, so it can pinpoint its prey

Females are brown all over; males have a grey-blue head

KESTREL
32–39 cm

Hovering as if suspended on a string, the kestrel is well adapted to hunting over urban ground. You may also see one perched on an overhead wire, building ledge, or bare treetop.

Head, eye, bill, and legs are all black

White eye and black cap with a grey neck

CARRION CROW
48–52 cm

Surprisingly large and bold close-up, this is our most familiar crow. It has a loud, harsh call and, unlike the similar-looking rook, is not often found in large flocks.

JACKDAW
34–39 cm

This small grey-black crow nests in buildings, chimneys, and holes in trees. Watch for the aerial acrobatics of their flocks, and listen for the loud, repetitive "kya" calls.

Rocky shores, cliffs, and open sea

A big seabird colony is alive with noise and movement – it even smells different. Add the open sea and the sky and you have one of the most exciting places to birdwatch.

Seabird cities

Craggy shorelines are harsh places, yet invaluable for nesting seabirds. Flat rocks, ledges, and deep cavities attract different species, all of which feed out at sea but must find a safe place to lay their eggs.

On cliffs and islands you may see cormorants, shags, and gulls – including the kittiwake, a genuine "seagull". Perhaps you will find fulmars and an assortment of auks: guillemots (on ledges); razorbills (often in natural cavities); and puffins (nesting in deeper burrows). These auks lay eggs directly onto bare rock, while kittiwakes build bulky nests in rows. Cliffs become white with droppings by midsummer.

In cavities and old rabbit holes there may be petrels and Manx shearwaters, which cannot walk and come to the nest only after dark. You might need to book an organized expedition to see those, but they are often visible offshore in the daytime.

Between the rocks, there may be patches of shoreline, which can be covered in weed. This offers places for some waders to feed, but the numbers and variety are never as high as you'll see on muddy coasts.

On the rock face

Coastal cliffs are a key stronghold for the agile, powerful peregrine falcon, which breeds high on the rocky ledges.

Expert divers

Gathering in huge, noisy colonies on coastal rocks, gannets feed on fish, diving head-first into the sea to catch their food.

Hardy waders

Purple sandpipers can be seen picking over seaweed-covered rocks in search of crustaceans and molluscs to eat.

Bird stacks
In the breeding season, rock "stacks" can be completely taken over by noisy colonies of nesting seabirds.

Black plumage becomes mottled in winter

Brown head turns white with dark stripe in winter

GUILLEMOT
32–38 cm

Often seen upright, squatting on a ledge, this bird is buoyant on the water, with a whirring, heavy flight over the water.

Back is grey-brown with curled whitish fringes

BLACK GUILLEMOT
34 cm

Look for these on rocky islets, not sheer cliffs. Pairs bob around inshore or sit on rocks, revealing bright red legs.

PURPLE SANDPIPER
21 cm

A small, dark bird with dull yellow legs, this wader visits in winter to feed on weedy, wave-splashed rocks and drifts of seaweed.

RAZORBILL
37–39 cm

This bird typically shares breeding colonies with guillemots, but prefers the shady cavities. In winter, their black heads turn white with a black cap, and some stay near the shore.

Thick black bill with white lines

Red bill and legs, with black plumage

CHOUGH
37–42 cm

Found on cliffs and ledges, this crow is acrobatic in flight and flicks its wings as it feeds. Its name is pronounced "chuff" but its call is a loud "chow".

Two black bars on a pale wing

FERAL PIGEON/ ROCK DOVE
29–37 cm

Like the familiar town pigeon, these feral birds vary in colour and pattern, but truly wild rock doves are now rare.

Pale stripe over eye and under cheek

ROCK PIPIT
16–17 cm

Distinguished by dark legs, this small bird has a yellowish underside with blurred streaks. Find it feeding among the stones of rocky beaches.

KITTIWAKE
40 cm

This pretty gull spends all winter at sea, then nests on sheer cliffs and ledges. Its loud "kiti-a-waake" call rings around the rocks.

White below, with silvery-grey upper parts

Black triangle on wingtip

FULMAR
102–122 cm

Although it resembles a medium-sized gull, the stiff-winged, grey-tailed fulmar is unrelated. It nests on rocky cliffs but is otherwise to be found at sea.

Thick bill has tubular nostrils

Sharp-edged translucent wings

ARCTIC TERN
30–39 cm

An elegant bird with a long tail, very short red legs, and a blood-red beak, this tern nests on shingle or rocks, but will dive-bomb intruders, so keep your distance!

Birds of rocky shores, cliffs, and open sea

Look offshore for birds flying low over the sea, moving to and from their feeding areas, or in the nooks and crannies along the shoreline. In spring, train your binoculars on the rocky cliffs to spot the nesting sites.

SHAG
78 cm

See the shag diving for food and swimming in rolling surf – or perched on a rock with wings outspread to dry out its feathers, which are not waterproof.

Snake-like neck, tufty crest, and slender bill

Dark head and black moustache, with white cheeks

PEREGRINE
34–58 cm

This bird of prey nests on cliffs and roams widely in search of food, soaring with short bursts of quick, stiff wingbeats.

Slightly smaller than a cormorant, with all-dark plumage

Distinctive yellow head

GANNET
87–100 cm

A goose-sized seabird with a gleaming white body and long, black-tipped wings, it can be found in huge, noisy, crowded colonies on cliffs.

Black above and white below

Grey face edged with black cap and neck

MANX SHEARWATER
30–37 cm

A migrant that travels thousands of miles to nest in island burrows, this seabird has such weak legs it cannot stand or walk, but flies out at night to fish for food.

Colourful bill to attract a mate

PUFFIN
29–34 cm

Waddling on orange legs, the puffin nests in burrows rather than on open cliff ledges and spends winter at sea

Take care of your binoculars – keep them dry and protected from salty sea spray

Winter aerobatics
Dunlins roost together on the shoreline in their thousands at high tide. If you're lucky, you might see aerobatic displays as flocks arrive to roost.

Sandy shores

Many birds live in shallow offshore bays and along sandy
shorelines, often fringed by grass-covered dunes, but
beaches can be too busy with human activity, so most
nesting birds are found on nature reserves.

Open spaces and big skies

Although wide, sandy beaches have fewer birds of fewer kinds compared with muddy
estuaries, you'll still find plenty of action on land and in the air. On the shores there
may be ringed plovers nesting, and common, little, and Sandwich terns.

From autumn to spring, you'll see visiting waders, particularly sanderlings, dunlins,
turnstones, and oystercatchers. They and many other birds may choose a coastal lagoon
as their high-tide roost, and flocks should not be disturbed while they're resting, but
you can probably get a good view from the dunes with a scope or binoculars.

Down at the water's edge, sanderlings dart in and out with the waves, while
turnstones flip over seaweed and pebbles along the strandline to hunt for food beneath.
These waterline birds, too, are sensitive to disturbance and need to be left in peace if
they are to nest successfully. Sanderlings are absent only in midsummer, which is also
when the terns are away, feeding offshore.

Look offshore to see diving ducks feeding on shellfish, such as eiders, common
scoters, and, in winter, perhaps long-tailed ducks. Often they appear only as the
swell rises, or when they fly low over the waves in straggling lines.

On the waterline
When not roosting in tight flocks,
pearl-and-silver winter sanderlings
can be seen feeding at speed,
running along the water's edge.

Handsome gulls
Although black-headed gulls
nest on marshes, you can see
them feeding on sandy beaches,
striking in their summer plumage.

Offshore swimmers
Look for common scoters
swimming just offshore. Male
scoters are black, but the browner
females have a pale face.

AVOCET
42–46 cm

Upturned bill sweeps sideways through the water to feed

A specialist of shallow coastal lagoons, this slender long-legged wader is found on sandy shores, estuaries, and mudflats.

BAR-TAILED GODWIT
37–41 cm

Look for this tall wader on the waterline at low tide. It is especially common in winter, when its brown-grey summer plumage turns streaky grey with white underparts.

Long bill is very slightly upcurved

Dark patch on shoulder

SANDERLING
18–20 cm

Watch this little twinkle-toed wader as it runs along the tideline, dodging waves and looking for food.

Black legs

Bushy black crest

Long black bill with yellow tip

Slim, elegant bill is faintly uptilted

RED-THROATED DIVER
53–69 cm

Roughly the size of a mallard, this bird is often on the water, or flying low with its long neck extended and feet trailing.

Short tail with no swallow-like streamers

Pale wings and very pale body

SANDWICH TERN
36–41 cm

If you're lucky, you might spot this large, angular summer visitor as it pauses over the sea before diving headlong into the water with a striking splash to catch a fish.

COMMON TERN
31–38 cm

This widespread, medium-sized tern has a pointed orange bill with a black tip. It does not walk easily on its short red legs, but hovers over the water before diving for fish.

Long tail streamers resemble a swallow's in flight

Yellow bill and white forehead

LITTLE TERN
21–25 cm

The smallest, fastest tern, this bird is agile in the air and feeds with a headlong vertical plunge and noticeable "smack" into the sea, often close inshore.

Check when high tide is, to make sure you don't get stranded

GREAT BLACK-BACKED GULL
64–79 cm

Our largest gull, with a massive head and bill, this bird is majestic and powerful in flight, with long glides on bowed wings.

Legs are dull pale pink

Adult male has a long black tail, absent in females

LONG-TAILED DUCK
50–60 cm

The plumage of this winter visitor changes over the season and flocks will be a busy mix of dark and light birds. They fly low over the sea, flock on the water, and dive for food.

Bright orange legs

TURNSTONE
20–25 cm

Find this bird on the beach, rolling over pebbles and weed to unearth the food beneath, and chattering with quick, sharp calls.

SHELDUCK
55–65 cm

A striking, boldly piebald duck that is almost as big as a goose, the shelduck feeds on open beaches or in sheltered creeks.

COMMON SCOTER
43–54 cm

Found in flocks offshore, or flying in long, undulating lines low over the sea, this large, dark duck is bulky but elegant.

RED-BREASTED MERGANSER
51–64 cm

A frequent diver and efficient hunter of fish, this large, elongated, angular duck gathers in groups or larger flocks offshore.

Long, serrated bill is good for gripping fish

SHORELARK
14–17 cm

You may see this relatively rare winter visitor, with its striking face markings and black "horns", on open beach or beside shallow, sandy streams.

Bill is orange and black

RINGED PLOVER
19 cm

Their distinctive foraging technique – a "run-stop-tilt forward" feeding action – helps you identify plovers. This plover is boldly marked on the head and breast.

Male is black and white; female is brown ♀

EIDER
50–70 cm

A large, wedge-billed seaduck, the eider favours wide bays and mussel beds, diving for food; it is often found in flocks.

Birds of sandy shores

Sandy beaches, bays, and coastal lagoons are often used by people, but some birds manage to thrive too. Visit at low tide, when the birds are feeding on the exposed strandline, or as the incoming tide pushes flocks up to the high-water mark.

Estuaries

Estuaries combine several habitats, each offering opportunities for watching different birds through the year. Be careful not to disturb resting flocks at high tide, and also to keep safe in areas with fast-rising water and deep muddy creeks.

Wide, open spaces

Large estuaries may have thousands of birds, but they can be spread out across this big, broad habitat, so timing can make a huge difference to how many of them you actually see. Try to time your visits for an incoming tide, when you'll see the birds move from feeding areas to roosts. You will see dense flocks of many species, but as the tide falls again they disperse and become harder to identify from a distance. At low tide you'll see waders combing the mudflats in search of crustaceans, molluscs, and worms.

Listen to the calls. Waders nearly always call in flight, making identification so much easier. In winter, the chatter of huge flocks of geese fills the air, and wildfowl may join in the daily movements, coming to the saltmarsh to roost and moving off to feed, sometimes inland (as with geese) or out at the water's edge. At dusk, flocks of pink-footed geese create wonderful spectacles against evening skies.

In summer, estuarine marshes may have breeding black-headed gulls, redshanks, and lapwings. And, if they are not disturbed by humans and predators, you may see ringed plovers, gulls, and terns nesting on sandbars and shingle ridges.

Ready to breed

In spring, before heading north to breed, knots develop a rich "red" breeding plumage.

Unique beak

In the shallows, avocets sweep their upcurved bill sideways through the water to detect food.

Winter geese

Although several species of geese use the marsh, the brent goose is the one that feeds out on the mudflats.

Hustle and bustle
Flocks of black-tailed godwits create peculiar buzzing notes as well as loud flight calls when settling to feed or roost in shallow water.

Birds of estuaries

On the water you may see gulls and perhaps diving ducks and grebes, while marshes and muddy creeks will have more waders, ducks, and geese. At low tide, look for waders on the mudflats too.

♀

Male has brown head with white neck-stripe

WIGEON
42–52 cm

This medium-sized, short-legged dabbling duck is often found in large flocks on grassy saltmarsh, grazing like tiny, colourful geese.

♀

PINTAIL
51–62 cm

Out on the saltmarsh you may see the elegant, long-necked pintail, a quiet dabbling duck. Look for the white breast and long tail of the males.

Males have pink breast and chestnut-coloured head

WHITE-FRONTED GOOSE
64–78 cm

White markings on the forehead and around the bill give this winter visitor its name. Flocks fly in long lines and V-shapes, with a loud, yodelling chorus.

Pale breast contrasts with dark head

PINK-FOOTED GOOSE
60–75 cm

As well as the distinctive pink legs, this relatively small, pale goose has a short neck and small bill. Flocks fly in long lines and V-shapes with a babbling chorus.

Black bars across the belly

BRENT GOOSE
55–60 cm

The smallest goose to visit in winter, this bird has a black neck and head, and flies with distinctive low, guttural calls.

Orange legs

Black wings, back, and head

BARNACLE GOOSE
55–70 cm

A boldly marked, handsome goose, this overwintering bird feeds on marsh or pasture. Flocks often fly in straggly lines and create a dog-like, yapping chorus.

White belly below black "breastplate"

Underside is dull brown or whitish

GREENSHANK
30–35 cm
Dull green legs and greyer colours distinguish this wader from the redshank. It likes muddy creeks at the edges of estuaries.

BLACK-TAILED GODWIT
36–44 cm
Often found in muddy creeks rather than on open beaches, this large, long-legged wader has bold white wingbars in flight.

Legs are longer than a bar-tailed godwit's

DUNLIN
16–22 cm
Probing for food with its slender bill, the little dunlin has a grey winter plumage (shown) that becomes brighter in spring, with a rectangular black belly patch.

REDSHANK
28 cm
Often the noisiest wader with "bouncy", repetitive calls, the redshank feeds in shallow estuary waters and mudflats.

SPOTTED REDSHANK
29–33 cm
Larger than a redshank but also with bright red legs, this slender wader is pale in autumn/winter, and blackish in spring.

Slender bill is longer than a redshank's

CURLEW
50–60 cm
Mottled brown and buff, this large wader has a distinctive bill and unmistakeable "cur-lee" call.

Long, downcurved bill for probing the mud

WHIMBREL
40–57 cm
Slightly smaller than a curlew, the whimbrel has a striped head and quick, trilling call note. In spring, flocks pass offshore or rest on saltmarsh.

GREY PLOVER
27–30 cm
This winter visitor has a dull, mottled grey plumage that turns speckled silver-and-black in spring. Listen for its distinctive "teeoo-ee" calls.

Silver-grey plumage with white underneath

KNOT
25–30 cm
With its shortish bill and legs, this medium-sized chunky wader can be spotted in winter, often in dense flocks that perform spectacular manoeuvres in flight.

OYSTERCATCHER
40–50 cm
Easy to see and identify, with its bold black-and-white pattern, this wader has a very distinctive loud, piping call.

White throat band in winter

Pinky-red legs

Bright red bill is pointed or chisel-tipped

Stay on the paths to avoid marshy ground – and, in spring, to make sure you don't disturb any nesting birds

Rivers

From silvery trickles of cold water in the uplands, to rushing torrents over rocky riverbeds, to slow, meandering waterways nearing the sea, rivers offer a varied set of habitats to suit many different types of birds.

Different speeds for different species

As rivers make their way from their source, they commonly flow over different soils and rocks, gathering speed and then perhaps slowing as they broaden out. They will support a variety of vegetation, invertebrates, and fish along the way – and beside their banks will be birds hunting among those food sources. Few birds can adapt to them all, so visit a range of rivers to fully explore the species that make rivers their home.

Upland streams can be good in summer, with beautifully crystal-clear waters that have been filtered through chalk and limestone. Common sandpipers nest alongside them. You may see dippers there too, or down on lower reaches, as long as they are clean, fast-flowing, and fringed with trees or rocks. This unique songbird feeds underwater, even walking on the river bottom.

Kingfishers are expected but often overlooked, remarkably inconspicuous in the dappled waterside light. Listen for their high, sharp calls as they fly by. Another giveaway call is the sharp note of the grey wagtail. Only broad, still stretches of river are used by fish-eating goosanders and great crested grebes, but you can find little grebes on smaller rivers. Look to the slow-moving edges of larger rivers to see grey herons patiently waiting for fish to swim within range.

Riverbank nests
In spring, look for nests of the goosander in riverside trees. When very young, chicks hitch a ride on their mother's back.

Waterside wagtails
By the river you'll see grey wagtails; they have a longer, slimmer tail than the yellow wagtail, which prefers nearby pastureland.

Stalking the shallows
You'll find the little egret patrolling the edges of slow rivers, hunting perhaps for crustaceans, small fish, or reptiles.

A flash of colour
On a branch overhanging a river, you may spot a kingfisher patiently watching and waiting. If you're lucky, you might see it dive for a minnow.

KINGFISHER
17–19 cm

Perched immobile on a branch over the river, the kingfisher waits for its moment to dive in and catch a fish. Look for it flying low over water with a flash of its vivid back.

Copper-coloured underparts

Bright blue upper body

Especially long black-and-white tail

GREY WAGTAIL
18–19 cm

A beautiful flash of yellow underparts mark this slender bird, which has a grey back and a white band along its underwing.

White stripe above the eye

SEDGE WARBLER
13 cm

Look among reeds or willow to see this summer visitor. Males have a hugely varied song repertoire.

SAND MARTIN
12 cm

A brown band across the breast and a short forked tail distinguishes this tiny summer visitor, which nests in burrows it tunnels into riverbanks.

REED BUNTING
16 cm

A white collar helps you identify this little streaky brown bird, often found in reedbeds.

Slender long neck

Brown head with greyer back

Droopy crest feathers and black eyestripe

Grey upper parts

White bib and chestnut breast band

Yellow feet below dark legs

DIPPER
17–20 cm

Preferring clean, fast streams with rocks or trees alongside, this plump little bird wades, swims, dives for food – and can even walk under water.

Dagger-like yellow bill

LITTLE EGRET
55–65 cm

Pure-white with a black bill, this small heron develops wispy plumes in the breeding season. It is often inactive but is lively and quick when it spots a meal.

GREY HERON
84–102 cm

The bright white neck of this very large bird is typically sunk into its shoulders; in flight, its broad, arched wings flap languidly and its long legs stretch out behind.

Swallow-like forked tail in flight

COMMON TERN
31–38 cm

A widespread tern with a pointed orange bill and short legs. It clusters in noisy flocks and plunges into the water to catch fish.

Stands immobile in the shallows, waiting for prey

Birds of rivers

Over fast-flowing waters you may see little insect-feeding birds darting around, while the waders, divers, and dabbling waterfowl are at home on slower waters. Increasingly, the cormorant is making its home inland too.

White underside curves up in front of wing

COMMON SANDPIPER
19–21 cm
Preferring fast-flowing rivers, this small, sandy-brown, dull-legged wader bobs and swings its tail up and down.

LITTLE GREBE
23–29 cm
On larger rivers you may see this small, round, buoyant waterbird. Mostly afloat rather than on land, it dives from the surface to feed.

Almost tailless, fluffy rounded end

CORMORANT
100 cm
You may find this very large, glossy, black waterbird standing on a riverbank, perhaps stretching out its wings to dry them after diving in for a fish.

Hook-tipped bill for catching fish

Male has glossy green breeding plumage

MALLARD
50–65 cm
The familiar orange-legged duck: males are brightly coloured, females are streaky-brown; both have a blue wing patch.

Female has a slightly crested, reddish-brown head

GOOSANDER
58–68 cm ♀
This large, streamlined duck has a serrated bill, good for gripping the fish it dives to catch. It nests in holes in trees and swims low in the water or rests on the bank, revealing red legs.

From source to sea, one river alone can offer a huge range of habitats for birds

Freshwater marshes

In these permanently damp or flooded places, specialist vegetation develops, along with birds highly adapted to living on, around, and above the water margins.

Hide and seek

The edge of a reedbed is a varied and rewarding place for birds and birdwatcher alike. Dense wetland vegetation often thins out at the edge, with little openings, ditches, and streams in the reeds, grass, and sedge. These allow in light for other plants and insects, while also offering cover for fish-eating birds to hide and let the fish come to them.

Look in the dense foliage of reedbeds or nearby willows for summer migrants such as small warblers. They may be joined by familiar acrobatic species such as wrens and blue tits. On the waterline beneath, moorhens will feed, alongside water rails and bitterns, although you're more likely to hear than see these elusive marsh-dwellers, as their plumage camouflages them perfectly and they hide deep among the reed stems. In winter, starlings crowd into dense vegetation over water to keep safe and warm at night.

Reed camouflage
Hidden in the reedbeds are birds such as bitterns; visit in spring to hear the deep, booming call of the males.

Reed seed-eaters
Listen for "pinging" calls and look for rustling stems to see the bearded tit, which is specially adapted to live only in reedbeds.

Reedbed predator
Other birds of prey and owls feed over reedbeds, but the marsh harrier is the specialist that nests within them.

Birds that rely on reedbeds are naturally rare and localized. Bearded tits, for example, feed and nest only within reeds, while some long-toed birds wade within the thick cover. In extensive reedbeds, rare bitterns may breed, then wander in winter back to smaller sites with shallow water within the marsh vegetation. Marsh harriers can exploit small patches of reedbed and feed over adjacent open ground.

Gigantic roosts
Starling roosts in reedbeds can number millions, and at dusk they may put on spectacular flight displays ("murmurations") before they finally settle.

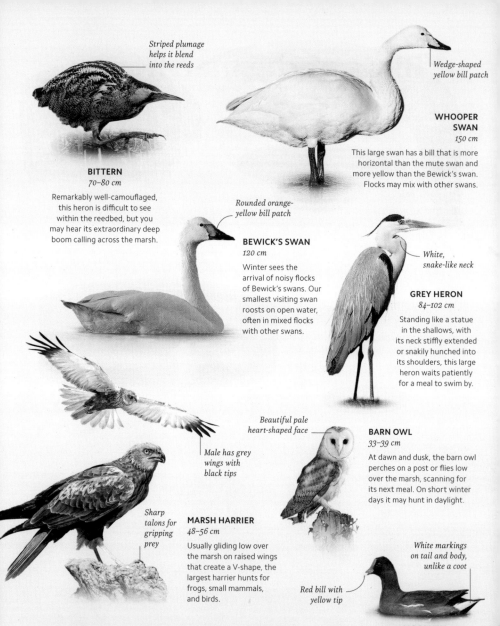

Striped plumage helps it blend into the reeds

Wedge-shaped yellow bill patch

WHOOPER SWAN
150 cm

This large swan has a bill that is more horizontal than the mute swan and more yellow than the Bewick's swan. Flocks may mix with other swans.

BITTERN
70–80 cm

Remarkably well-camouflaged, this heron is difficult to see within the reedbed, but you may hear its extraordinary deep boom calling across the marsh.

Rounded orange-yellow bill patch

BEWICK'S SWAN
120 cm

Winter sees the arrival of noisy flocks of Bewick's swans. Our smallest visiting swan roosts on open water, often in mixed flocks with other swans.

White, snake-like neck

GREY HERON
84–102 cm

Standing like a statue in the shallows, with its neck stiffly extended or snakily hunched into its shoulders, this large heron waits patiently for a meal to swim by.

Beautiful pale heart-shaped face

BARN OWL
33–39 cm

At dawn and dusk, the barn owl perches on a post or flies low over the marsh, scanning for its next meal. On short winter days it may hunt in daylight.

Male has grey wings with black tips

Sharp talons for gripping prey

MARSH HARRIER
48–56 cm

Usually gliding low over the marsh on raised wings that create a V-shape, the largest harrier hunts for frogs, small mammals, and birds.

White markings on tail and body, unlike a coot

Red bill with yellow tip

MOORHEN
30–38 cm

Unlike the similar coot, the moorhen has a red bill and white markings on its tail and body. You may see it on the water or beside it.

Watch the "inbetween" spaces
where water and vegetation meet
– that's where many birds like to hide

Birds of the marshes

Freshwater marshes come to life with warblers and wagtails in summer, but the winter wildfowl can also be exciting. Look amongst the reeds and waterline vegetation for signs of activity.

Male has a black "moustache"

White collar and "moustache"

REED BUNTING
13–15 cm

Look for this little bird perching upright on a stem or feeding on open ground. The male has a black head, while the female's head is brown with dark cheeks.

BEARDED TIT
14–15 cm

Check for giveaway movements of reed stems to find this striking little bird. The female has a plain sandy-brown head, but the male has a distinctive "moustache".

REED WARBLER
13 cm

It can be hard to spot this slender tiny warbler hiding in dense reeds, but you may hear its rhythmic churring song.

SEDGE WARBLER
13 cm

Often found in rougher, more varied, vegetation than the reed warbler, this bird's song is also more varied – musical and chattering, with a less regular rhythm.

YELLOW WAGTAIL
15–16 cm

A summer visitor, this small bird is often found darting around on the damp ground, wagging its tail and chasing insects.

Male has brighter yellow belly than female

Short, slightly downcurved bill

RUFF
25–34 cm

Feeding in the shallow waters of marshes, this medium-sized wader is generally pale brown, but in spring breeding males develop a colourful ruff and crest.

WATER RAIL
23–28 cm

Hiding in the waterside vegetation is this shy, round, red-billed bird, creeping on flexed legs. You're more likely to hear its pig-like squeals than see it.

Long, straight bill for unearthing worms

JACK SNIPE
18–25 cm

A winter visitor, this very small, dark snipe is hard to see, as it hides in dense vegetation and generally only flies up if disturbed.

SNIPE
25–27 cm

Hiding at the water's edge or in dense vegetation, this medium-sized wader is camouflaged by brown and cream stripes on its head and back.

Dark brown back with gold stripes

Lakes, reservoirs, and gravel pits

Natural lakes, flooded gravel pits, and reservoirs all offer wetland bird habitats that often have hides built beside them, so you can watch the birds without disturbing them.

Sit and watch

Wetland areas lend themselves to permanent public hides, which gives you the benefit of shelter, a little comfort, and a good view, while also reducing disturbance to the local bird population. Wildfowl and waders at the water's edge are prone to fly off and never return, so keeping still and watching from a fixed point can be particularly important here.

Out on the water, you may see grebes, cormorants, and a variety of ducks, usually grouped into diving ducks and surface-feeders (or "dabbling" ducks). Some dabblers, such as wigeon, also feed on adjacent grassland and often rest on the bank. In winter,

Expert fisher
In summer, keep an eye on the skies over the water for an osprey hunting for fish.

At the water's edge
If you see a small, dark wader with a glistening white underside, it may be a green sandpiper.

Scooping up food
Out on the water, the shoveler's broad bill is adapted to sieve food from near the water's surface.

both number and variety are greatly increased. Start at one end and scan through the flocks to see what you can find. Lakes also serve as night-time roosts for thousands of gulls, especially in winter. Even when these water habitats are far inland, if the water levels are low, migrant waders such as greenshanks, common and green sandpipers, sanderlings, dunlins, and ringed plovers will be attracted to them, especially in spring and autumn.

Rites of courtship
See great crested grebes perform their ritualized mating "dance" in spring, displaying their beautiful crest and ruff and doing co-ordinated dives.

POCHARD ♀
45 cm

Sleepy and inactive by day, this diving duck feeds largely at night. Large numbers flock to overwinter on lakes and reservoirs.

Male breeding plumage is dark both ends, pale in the middle

Male has tuft on nape of neck

♀

Male has striking black-and-white plumag[e]

♀

SMEW
38–44 cm

A great diver, this small, sleek duck is a rare winter visitor. The male is mostly white, but females and juveniles have a red-brown head.

TUFTED DUCK
40–45 cm

Often inactive on the water, this small diving duck has a tuft on its head. The male is black-and-white; the female is chocolate-brown.

Male has green sheen on its head

♀

Shovel-like bill for feeding on water surface

GOLDENEYE
45 cm

Less likely to be found in flocks than other ducks, this medium-sized diving duck has a short, triangular bill. Females are grey and brown, while males are more striking.

SHOVELER
44–50 cm

A large, heavy-headed dabbling duck, the shoveler "sweeps" its bill through the water to feed on plant matter and invertebrates.

Impressive crest and ruff in summer

Winter plumage lacks crest and ruff

Bright green wing patch

♀

TEAL
30–41 cm

Overwintering in large flocks, this pretty, small, dark-legged duck is agile in flight. Both male and female have a bright green patch on their hindwing.

GREAT CRESTED GREBE
46–51 cm

A diving waterbird unable to walk on land, this grebe nests at the water's edge. During the breeding season it grows a striking ruff for an ornate mating display.

♀

GADWALL
47–58 cm

More commonly spotted in winter, this large dabbling duck is relatively plain, but both male and female have a white patch on the wing.

Distinct white diamond on hindwing

Birds of lakes, reservoirs, and gravel pits

Many landbirds are drawn to drink or feed over and around lakes, while "edge" habitats such as shoreline shingle, mud or grass, and reeds and willow thickets, all add variety for waterbirds.

SAND MARTIN
12–13 cm

Arriving in spring to nest and breed in tunnels it burrows into banks, this tiny brown-and-white bird swoops low over water to feed on small insects.

Forked tail

Black bill and yellow eyering

LITTLE RINGED PLOVER
15–18 cm

Gravel pits are perfect for this small, round, short-billed summer migrant. Smaller than the ringed plover, it has the same run-stop-tilt feeding action.

GREEN SANDPIPER
20–24 cm

See this medium-sized wader feeding on the shoreline. It has a darker back than other sandpipers, and is bright white below.

Watch from a hide to see a wide range of birds going about their daily life

BLACK TERN
25 cm

Here in the summer, this small, elegant tern has a black head and belly, with grey wings. It typically flies low over the water to catch insects.

OSPREY
43–60 cm

Perched high on a branch over the water, or hovering and diving for fish, this large summer visitor is an impressive sight.

Black stripe behind eye

Dark brown upper parts and white underparts

Narrow black "moustache"

HOBBY
29–36 cm

This small falcon can be seen in summer as it circles, rises, and "stalls" to catch insects in flight. It has long, pointed wings, and a white throat and cheeks.

Hooked bill for catching fish

Long, serpentine neck

CORMORANT
100 cm

This bird dives and swims for fish, then perches on a post or rock to dry out its feathers, which are not waterproof. It has a distinctive profile, and a glossy black plumage and long tail.

The song of a lark
Skylarks sing at their flowing best in their high song-flights, but you may also hear them on a low bush or other perch.

Farmland, hedgerows, and grassland

The birds you see in this habitat will vary with the seasons and the rhythms of the farming calendar. Much depends too on local farming practices, which may leave bird populations vulnerable.

Adapting to change

By its very nature farmland changes through the year, as seeds are spread, grass is cut, and crops are harvested. But birds have had to adjust to even greater changes in farming practices, which have had a very significant impact. Some farmland species – particularly ground-nesting ones – have declined enormously as a result, such as redshanks, curlews, and lapwings. Winter flocks that were once a frequent sight have also gone, so you're less likely to see mixed flocks of finches, sparrows, and buntings. Even the change from spring-sown cereals to winter wheat, which is already tall and dense by spring, has reduced breeding opportunities for once-common birds such as skylarks and cuckoos.

There is still much to see in farmland habitats, however, especially if hedges have been retained and wildlife-friendly farming practices are in use. Look for gulls following the plough on arable land, and pheasant, partridge, and geese patrolling the fields for seeds, grains, and grasses. Flocks of fieldfares and redwings invade early-winter hedgerows and close-cropped pastures, with red kite hovering overhead, hunting for small mammals to eat. An isolated old oak is a good place to find a little owl – but you must find a rare rough, unimproved grassy meadow to hope for a hunting barn owl.

Nesting on the ground	Turning up worms	In the hedges
Although lapwings have nested on farm fields for centuries, modern farming practices put them at risk.	Large flocks of mixed gulls follow the plough as it turns the soil and offers up worms to eat.	Fieldfares arrive in October and eagerly devour the autumn crop of hedgerow berries.

Birds of farmland, hedgerows, and grassland

Although numbers have decreased in recent decades, there's still a variety of birdlife, often feeding on seeds and insects, or predating the smaller mammals sharing the space.

Grey bill, unlike the carrion crow

ROOK
45–47 cm

A superb flier that can soar very high, this large crow is black, glossy, and sociable, gathering in colonies called "rookeries" and flocking with jackdaws on fields.

Fluffy feathers around the legs

WOOD PIGEON
38–45 cm

A big, heavy pigeon with white markings on its neck and wings, this common bird has a repetitive "tu-too, too, tootoo, tu too, too, tu" call.

White neck patch and pink chest

Striking pink-red breast on males

BULLFINCH
14–17 cm

Often found in pairs, this plump little black-capped finch is a striking bird, especially the male (the female has a grey-brown breast).

Shimmering patch of green on the neck

STOCK DOVE
30–34 cm

This small grey pigeon lacks the white patches of the wood pigeon. It has a deep, cooing "oo-rrr-oo, oo-rrr-ooo" call.

Finely barred neck patch

Plain head and large, pale beak

LAPWING
28–31 cm

If you hear a "peewit" call, it's this uniquely crested black-and-white plover. In winter you may see flocks of them wheeling in the sky.

CORN BUNTING
16–19 cm

Perched on a wire or bush top, this starling-sized, finch-like, light-brown bird is quite a rare sight. It has a song like jingled keys or splintering glass.

TURTLE DOVE
25–27 cm

Colourful, slender, and rare, this summertime dove is patterned orange and brown on its back and has a soft, purring song.

LITTLE OWL
22 cm

Perched on a branch or stump, this small owl is mainly nocturnal but may hunt by day. It has pale eyes and distinctive "eyebrows".

PHEASANT
70–150 cm

A common sight on open land, this large gamebird is noisy when startled. The male is very colourful, with long tail feathers, while the females are speckled brown.

Black eyes set in white face

RED KITE
60–66 cm

A spectacular sight as it flies slowly over fields scanning for prey, this imposing bird has a deeply-notched tail and long, angled wings.

Orange face and striped back

Long, rust-red, forked tail

BARN OWL
32–40 cm

At dawn or dusk, you may see this medium-sized owl out on the prowl, flying low in search of prey. It has a white front and golden-sandy back.

Wings tipped with black

GREY PARTRIDGE
30–33 cm

Often prefering to run if disturbed, although it can fly fast and low, this small, round, short-tailed bird has stripes on its sides.

RED-LEGGED PARTRIDGE
30–35 cm

A plump, beautifully marked bird, it has stripes on its flanks and a white throat edged with black – and, of course, red legs.

COMMON GULL
40–46 cm

Playing fields and ploughed fields are the favoured habitat of this medium-sized gull. Silver-grey above, it has a white head and belly, and black wingtips.

Large orange bill

GREYLAG GOOSE
90 cm

Bulkier and shorter-necked than the Canada goose, this large, pale bird is often found in mixed flocks in fields.

Legs are pink or orange

Green-tinged legs

Reddish patches beneath the wings

Golden-yellow flush on upper breast

FIELDFARE
25 cm

A winter migrant that forms sociable flocks on pasture and berry-laden hedges, the fieldfare is a large thrush with a black-speckled breast.

REDWING
20 cm

Arriving for the winter to feast on hedgerow berries, this small, dark, sociable thrush has a striped face and streaky brown-and-cream markings.

BIRDS OF FARMLAND, HEDGEROWS, AND GRASSLAND **139**

Forests and woodland

What you see birdwatching in woodland depends on the season and place, but also the types of trees growing there. You will hear a lot more than you see, so listen and watch carefully.

Hiding and watching

Woodland birdwatching can be frustrating: you'll hear lots of birds, but they're often hidden by foliage, so you won't see as many as you hear. In late summer, even the best woods might seem empty, as birds wander in flocks or hide away during their annual moult. Which birds you'll encounter depends on the time of year and geographical location, but also the species and density of trees growing in the woodland.

Conifers have specialists such as crossbills, and adaptable birds such as great spotted woodpeckers. In places, localized species such as crested tits might appear. Even a conifer within a deciduous wood can attract the local coal tits and goldcrests. Old deciduous trees have familiar birds such as blackbirds, robins, and song thrushes. You may also see specialists such as pied flycatchers, wood warblers, and redstarts (a trio characteristic of western woods). Nightingales and willow tits prefer the dense, slender saplings of coppices.

In late summer, mixed flocks of blue, great, coal, and long-tailed tits attract nuthatches and other birds, too: by flocking with the tits they benefit from finding more food and seeing predators more quickly. And don't forget to look up for a sight of those predators, such as buzzards, sparrowhawks, and goshawks.

On tree trunks
You may hear a great spotted woodpecker before you see it, hunting for food under tree bark or chiselling out a nest hole.

Conifer specialist
Look on conifers for the crossbill, with its crossed bill tip and thick tongue to help prise open cones and extract seeds.

On the forest floor
Winter visitors such as bramblings feed on fallen seeds and beech mast on the woodland floor, often with chaffinches too.

In the trees
The classic woodland owl is this tawny owl – the one that hoots. In conifers and upland woodland you might find a long-eared owl.

GARDEN WARBLER
12 cm

This summer visitor prefers low trees and shrubs. It is very plain and you're more likely to hear its rich, flowing warble than see it.

Barred blue wing patch

Rounded wingtips

JAY
32–35 cm

In flight, this colourful crow appears largely black-and-white, but on a perch it reveals a beautiful pinkish plumage and irridescent blue patch.

Pure white underside

Long white oval on shoulder

WOOD WARBLER
11–12 cm

Look for this small warbler singing in the tree canopy, especially oak and beech. It has a green back and a yellow throat and eyestripe.

GREAT SPOTTED WOODPECKER
20–24 cm

Listen for the distinctive drumming of this medium-sized woodpecker in spring. It has striking black-and-white plumage, with a red flash under the tail.

Female is only slightly tinged with red

♀

TAWNY OWL
37–46 cm

Hunting by night, our largest owl may sometimes be spotted perched on a daytime roost, where it may be mobbed by small birds.

REDSTART
13–14.5 cm

In summer, scan oak copses or heathland for this robin-sized migrant, singing from the treetops. Males have a red breast and long red tail.

These juvenile streaks will develop into grey bars for the adult plumage

Black eyes in a round, brown face

SPARROWHAWK
28–38 cm

A relatively small hawk (the female is larger), this bird of prey has rounded wings and a slim tail. Their flight is more flap-and-glide than a kestrel's; they may soar but they never hover.

GOSHAWK
46–63 cm

Able to zoom through the trees at high speeds, this large hawk is a fearsome hunter. The larger female has whitish barred underparts; the smaller male's are more grey.

Birds of forests and woodland

Birds can be hard to spot in the depths of a wood, since they have to be alert and hide from phenomenal predators such as the "phantom of the forest", the goshawk.

Bold black
eyestripe

NUTHATCH
13–14 cm

Small and acrobatic,
this little bird can climb
headfirst up or down
trees, and its whistles
and trills carry far
through woods and
parkland.

*Mottled plumage for
perfect camouflage*

WOODCOCK
33–35 cm

Like a bulky nocturnal snipe,
the woodcock can be seen
flying over woods at dusk.
Its long, straight bill probes
the ground for worms.

Silvery-white underside

TREECREEPER
12.5 cm

Literally named, this
little bird creeps up
trees or hangs beneath
branches, hanging on
with long, curved claws.

*Bold white wedge
over eye, unlike
the goldcrest*

FIRECREST
9 cm

Along with the
goldcrest, this is our
tiniest bird, with even
brighter colours. Look
for it high up in holly
or ivy vegetation.

*Crossed bill
tip adapted
to feed on
cones*

♀

CROSSBILL
16.5 cm

This large finch flocks in conifers
to feed on the cones. Males are
red, while females are green.

*Female brown
and white*

♀

*White wing
patch*

PIED FLYCATCHER
12–13.5 cm

Arriving to breed in
summer, this small bird
nests in a tree hole or nestbox.
An insect-feeder, it flies out to
catch prey in the air, or
sometimes picks up food
from the ground.

Be patient, watch, and
listen for tell-tale signs
such as a branch jiggling,
or movement on a tree trunk

*Black cap and neat
little black chin*

MARSH TIT
12 cm

Often found near the edges of
woodland, this primarily brown tit
is very similar to the willow tit, but
its black cap is glossier, and its call
is a distinctive "pi-tchew".

Two pale wingbars

COAL TIT
9–10 cm

Tiny, rounded,
and acrobatic, this
bird lacks the bright
colours of other tits. It
likes conifers but can
be found in mixed
woodland too.

♀

*Male is yellow/
green; female has
black streaks*

SISKIN
12–13 cm

Listen for the distinctive squeaky calls and
buzzy, mechanical chatter from treetop
flocks of this tiny finch, often in larch or alder.

Heath, downs, and scrubland

The heather, gorse, and bracken that grow on heathland and chalk downs, often with an added layer of scrub habitat in the form of low, dense thickets, offer plenty of habitat and space for birds.

Big skies and broad landscapes

A walk on downs and heathland provides plenty of opportunities for birdwatching. Dry heath has stonechats, meadow pipits, and skylarks. If you're lucky, you might hear the distinctive sound of the cuckoo, and the beautiful song of the woodlark. Any tall trees might be used by tree pipits, with willow warblers and redpolls in the bushes.

Downland is more likely to have corn buntings and yellowhammers, and skylarks, as well as grey partridges and an assortment of crows. In places whinchats remain, although they have deserted many areas: they like high bracken slopes, young conifer plantations, and grassland with isolated tall stems. In patches of scrub, if you're very fortunate, you may encounter a relatively rare turtle dove or a singing nightingale,

Singing skylark
On the ground or in the air, the outpouring of song from a skylark may last for minutes on end.

Hiding in the heather
Meadow pipits are common, and will flit up from the ground with thin call notes as you pass.

Perched on gorse
Stonechats love gorse but can also be found on tall heather, fence posts, and overhead wires.

but you're more likely to find them being used by common and lesser whitethroats and a pair or two of bullfinches. Dunnocks and wrens are common here, as they are almost anywhere. Birds of prey soar overhead, preying on insects, small birds, and mammals. As well as the more common buzzards and red kites, you may see hobbies and maybe kestrels, although these are fewer than they once were.

Sharp-eyed hunter
Over open ground, look out for the distinctive hunting pattern of a hen harrier – a long, low glide on raised wings.

WHITETHROAT
14 cm

This summer migrant is a small, lively warbler. It sings from bush or wire or in flight, and has a puffy white throat and jerky tail.

Longer tail than lesser whitethroat

LESSER WHITETHROAT
13 cm

Smaller than its relative, with a dark patch on its cheek and a shorter tail, this reclusive greyish warbler hides in dense thickets and hedges.

Small crest can be raised

SKYLARK
18–19 cm

Hovering high over open ground, the skylark sings its distinctive, melodic song. It is ground-nesting, and is larger than a sparrow and smaller than a thrush.

WILLOW WARBLER
12 cm

Frequently found in summer in birch, willow, and other small trees on the edge of heathland, this little warbler has a sweet, descending song, unlike the repetitive "chiff-chaff" of the similar-looking chiffchaff.

Legs are paler than a chiffchaff's

Strong pale stripe over eye

WOODLARK
15–18 cm

Hard to spot, this small lark often keeps lookout in a tree, although it nests among grassy tussocks and heather scrub. Smaller than the skylark, it also has a shorter tail.

Grey-brown back with spotted belly

MISTLE THRUSH
27 cm

Larger than the similar-looking song thrush, this songbird likes tall trees, but can be found in heathland scrub.

Out on the open downs, listen out for the songs of the larks and pipits

Strong white eyestripe, unlike the stonechat

STONECHAT
12–14 cm

A small, plump, upright bird of heath and gorse, this bird has a "chat chat" call. It is darker than the whinchat, with no eyestripe.

Orange breast is paler on female

Male has black throat

WHINCHAT
12–14 cm

Unlike the resident stonechat, the whinchat is only here in summer. Lighter in colour, with a stripe over its eye, it likes tall grass, bracken, and upright stems.

Mottled plumage is excellent camouflage

NIGHTJAR
25–28 cm

Listen at dusk for the purring "churr" of this nocturnal insect-eate A summer migrant, it is typically wel hidden in heathland undergrowth.

Birds of heath, downs, and scrubland

Across these different types of habitat there is some overlap; heathland birds are not quite the same as downland ones, although several species are shared.

Red cap and black chin

REDPOLL
13–14 cm

Flocking in birch, alder, and pine, or feeding on seeds and insects in scrub, this small streaky brown finch has a distinctive red cap.

Juveniles are brown, turning greyer in adulthood

CUCKOO
32–34 cm

You're more likely to hear the famous "cu-coo" call of this summer migrant than spot the bird itself, hidden in the trees.

TREE PIPIT
14–15 cm

This summer visitor is often singing from the treetops, or on the ground (pipits always walk, never hop).

Flanks have weak streaks

Flanks have strong dark streaks

Male has black cheek; female is browner

WHEATEAR
14–15 cm

Find this small, ground-dwelling chat in summer on stony patches in grassland. It has a pale orange chest and white rump.

Streaky-brown with bright yellow head and belly

YELLOWHAMMER
16–16.5 cm

The male is much brighter yellow than the female. They have a distinctive "little-bit-of-bread-and-no-cheese" song.

MEADOW PIPIT
14–15 cm

In spring you may catch this small, streaky bird's fluttering "parachute" display flight, accompanied by a long trilling song.

BUZZARD
45–58 cm

Soaring high over the heath with its challenging "pi yar" call is this large, broad-winged, round-tailed bird of prey.

Dark breast above a pale band

Red cap and black moustache (red centre on male)

GREEN WOODPECKER
30–36 cm

This large olive-green woodpecker is often seen feeding on the ground, then flying up to a tree if disturbed. It has a loud, laughing call.

Mountain and moor

As moorland rises to become high, rugged hills and mountains, so too does the birdlife change. There are fewer species here than in other habitats, but they find a way to live in this wild terrain.

A harsh, beautiful environment

The foothills and low shoulders of mountains are often covered in moorland that then blends into rocky hills and peaks as the altitude increases and the treeline recedes. Birds are generally few in number and variety here, and those who make a home on rocky peaks and crags are different from the birds living on broad, rounded ridges.

Moors have large areas of rough grass, often with wet, boggy valleys and scattered hawthorns, or expanses of dark heather. Look for short-eared owls and hen harriers hunting over them, and meadow pipits almost everywhere, which in turn attract cuckoos. The latter lay eggs in the pipit's nest, letting the pipits do the hard work of rearing the cuckoo chicks. Deep gullies and crags may have ring ouzels, and patches of smooth grass close by are good for wheatears. Bracken and heather have whinchats, while in moorland/woodland edges you may see redstarts.

If you're going higher, do prepare sensibly for the weather and conditions. Look for ravens and, if you are in an area where there are golden eagles, scan the skyline, even at a great distance. A big brown bird of prey close up is likely to be a buzzard, but a distant dot could be an eagle and, who knows, it may come closer.

Perched high
In spring, look on cliff ledges and in tall trees to see the nests of the raven, a huge crow that behaves like a bird of prey.

At ground level
In summer, try to see the dotterel, a rare bird that lives on high, rolling ridges of broken rock, grasses, and moss.

On the rocks
A resident of the highest peaks, the ptarmigan has white wings and turns almost completely white in winter.

Apex predator
The mountains are eagle territory, and a glimpse of this fearsome hunter as it soars overhead is incredibly impressive.

Birds of mountain and moor

Unforgiving in winter, uplands in spring can become much busier as birds head up to breed. Few species are entirely mountain birds, but there are some that are characteristic of upland areas.

Golden head; darker on juveniles

Dark-brown upperparts fade in summer

GOLDEN EAGLE
66–100 cm

Huge and long-tailed, the golden eagle soars on broad, raised wings. Often at a great height, this magnificent bird of prey hunts over heath and moor, from lowland valleys to high peaks.

Large yellow feet have hooked black claws

White underparts in winter

GOLDEN PLOVER
26–29 cm

In spring this medium-sized plover moves upland to breed on open moor and high plateaus; in winter, it flocks on lowland fields and marshes.

Black beneath in summer, with speckled breeding plumage

MERLIN
24–33 cm

Floating on the breeze or flying fast and low, the merlin is a small, dynamic falcon of upland slopes, wooded gullies, and open moor.

Male is blue-grey above; female is brown

Female is brown, with a white rump

♀

Male is grey, with black wingtips

HEN HARRIER
41–52 cm

A large, slender bird of prey with long wings and tail, the hen harrier glides low over open ground on raised wings. You might also see it engaging in a tumbling display flight.

Long, pointed wings

RING OUZEL
24–27 cm

Like a blackbird but with pale wings and a white breastband, this thrush migrates here in summer to nest in cliffs, rocky gullies, and high moorland.

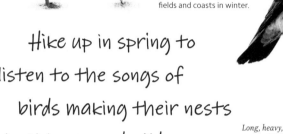

Juvenile plumage is mottled, with peachy underparts

Adult has coppery chest and white breastband

Strong white eyestripe

DOTTEREL
20–22 cm

Bold head stripes help identify this medium-small plover, which can be found breeding on high stony plateaus in spring, or on fields and coasts in winter.

Black "hood" on head

HOODED CROW
48–52 cm

A grey-bodied crow with a distinctive black head, tail, and wings. Where it shares habitat with carrion crows, it's common to find hybrid hooded × carrion crows.

Hike up in spring to listen to the songs of birds making their nests in this rugged wilderness

Long, heavy, arched bill

Pale round face and yellow eyes

SHORT-EARED OWL
35–43 cm

Unusually, this owl hunts by day, flying low over moor or marsh in search of voles. It is a large, pale, long-winged owl.

RAVEN
63–68 cm

Loud, croaking calls reveal the presence of this very large, all-black crow that feeds on carrion and nests on cliffs and in large trees.

Long, wedge-shaped tail

Longer wings than a barn owl

Red stripe above the eye

RED/WILLOW GROUSE
40 cm

Feeding on heather, this plump bird lives on upland heath and moorland. There are two subspecies: the native red grouse and the willow grouse of continental Europe, which has white wings.

BLACK GROUSE
45–60 cm

This is a large bird of the uplands. The long fan tail of the male is used in spring for a courtship display known as "lekking"; the female has a notched tail.

Grey-and-white camouflage in summer

Snow-white plumage in winter

Female is yellowish, with black stripes ♀

Fan tail is splayed during courtship

PTARMIGAN
30–34 cm

Living on rocky uplands in the far north, this mountain specialist has a bright red fleshy patch above the eye but otherwise blends into its habitat, turning white in winter.

Glossary

Adult A fully mature bird that is able to breed and in its final plumage.

Altricial A young bird that is helpless and dependent on its parents when it hatches.

Barred With marks that cross the body, wings, or tail.

Bird of prey A predatory carnivorous bird with acute eyesight, muscular legs, and sharp bill and talons.

Breeding plumage The plumage worn when birds display and pair.

Brood Young produced from a single clutch of eggs that are incubated together.

Call Vocal sound conveying a variety of messages, often particular to a single species.

Churring A repetitive trill, such as that produced at dusk by nightjars.

Clutch A group of eggs laid in a single nest, and incubated together.

Colony A group of the same species nesting together in the same area.

Covert A small feather in a well-defined tract on the wing or at the base of the tail, covering the base of the larger flight feathers.

Dabble To feed in shallow water by filtering water through the bill to remove food such as seeds, hence "dabbling duck".

Dawn chorus The short-lived concentration of birdsong around dawn, especially in spring.

Display Ritualized behaviour often used in courtship, to claim territory, or (as a distraction display) to lure a predator away from a nest.

Diving duck A species of duck that swims on the surface, from which it dives under to seek food.

Drumming An instrumental sound made by vibrating the bill against a branch (woodpeckers) or vibrating outspread tail feathers through the air (snipe).

Ear tuft A bunch of feathers on an owl's head that can be raised as a visual signal.

Eclipse Summer plumage of male ducks and some other species, to help camouflage them during their moult.

Eyebrow A line of colour above the eye and cheek (also known as a superciliary stripe).

Eye patch An area of colour around the eye.

Eyering A ring of colour around the eye.

Eyestripe A stripe of colour running in front of and behind the eye.

Feral Living wild, but derived from domestic stock that has escaped.

Fledge To leave the nest or acquire the first complete set of flight feathers; birds are known as fledglings.

Flight feathers A collective term for the large feathers on a bird's wing (primaries and secondaries).

Forewing The front part of the spread wing, including outer primaries, primary coverts, and smaller secondary coverts.

Hindwing The rear of the wing, including the inner primary feathers and the secondaries.

Immature Not yet fully adult or generally able to breed.

Incubate To keep eggs warm as they develop, until they hatch.

Inner wing The inner half of the wing, including the secondary coverts and secondaries.

Juvenile A bird in its first plumage, before it has its first moult.

Lek A gathering of birds at which the males display or fight to impress watching females before mating (without forming pairs).

Mottled Flecked with patches of colour.

Moult The shedding of old feathers and growth of new replacements in a systematic fashion that is characteristic of the species.

Moustache A stripe of colour from the base of the bill, beside the throat.

Migrant A species that spends part of the year in one geographical area and part in another, "migrating" between the two.

Orbital ring A thin, bare, fleshy ring around the eye, often of a distinctive colour.

Outer wing The outer half of the spread wing, including the primaries and primary coverts.

Plunge-diving Diving into water from the air, rather than a perch or the surface, to catch a fish.

Precocial A young bird that is well developed at hatching and soon able to fend for itself.

Preening Maintaining the feathers in good condition

by cleaning, smoothing, oiling, and lubricating them.

Primary One of the large outer wing feathers, growing from the digits.

Roost A place where birds sleep, or the act of sleeping.

Scapular One of a more or less oval tract of feathers growing from the shoulders, each side of the back.

Secondary One of the row of long, stiff feathers at the trailing edge of the inner wing.

Song A vocal performance with a pattern characteristic of the species; may attract a mate, or repel intruders from a territory.

Song-flight A special and usually distinctive flight in which the song is performed; often short (as in warblers), but sometimes prolonged (as in larks).

Species A group of living organisms, individuals of which can interbreed and produce fertile offspring, but which usually do not or cannot breed with individuals of other species.

Streaked Marked with lines of colour aligned lengthwise along the body.

Subspecies A more or less distinct group within a species, defined by geographical area; also "race".

Superciliary stripe A line of colour above the eye (also called the eyebrow).

Tail coverts (upper and under) Feathers covering the base of the tail.

Talon A claw (of a bird of prey).

Tarsus The longest, most obvious part of a bird's leg, between the "toes" and the "ankle joint" (often called the "knee", but points backwards).

Territory An area defended by a pair or individual, for breeding or feeding.

Tertial One of a small group of feathers at the base of the wing, adjacent to the innermost secondaries.

Wader A bird or species within a group of families, including plovers and sandpipers, which may or may not actually wade in water.

Waterfowl A loose term that includes wildfowl, crakes and rails, wading birds, and grebes.

Wildfowl A collective term specifically for ducks, geese, and swans.

Wingbar A line of colour across the coverts on the closed wing (as on a chaffinch), or along the extended wing as a bar or stripe (as on the tufted duck or ringed plover).

Next steps

USEFUL WEBSITES

On these websites you can find further information on birdwatching, sites to visit, local clubs to join, and much more.

Royal Society for the Protection of Birds (RSPB) The UK's largest nature conservation agency, with over 200 reserves in a wide range of habitats, many with bird hides and visitor centres. *www.rspb.org.uk*

British Trust for Ornithology (BTO) The BTO conducts population and breeding surveys; carries out bird-ringing, largely by volunteers; and manages BirdTrack, an online citizen science website. *www.bto.org*

Scottish Ornithologists' Club (SOC) The SOC provides information on birdwatching in Scotland, and is part of BirdTrack. *www.the-soc.org.uk*

Welsh Ornithological Society (Cymdeithas Adaryddol Cymru) It provides information on birdwatching in Wales, and is part of BirdTrack. *www.birdsinwales.org.uk*

Wildfowl & Wetlands Trust (WWT) A charity for the protection of wetland birds and their habitats, with ten reserves and visitor centres. *www.wwt.org.uk*

Wildlife Trusts The umbrella organisation for 46 local Wildlife Trusts that between them look after more than 2,300 nature reserves. *www.wildlifetrusts.org*

BirdWatch Ireland (BWI) An organization for the conservation and protection of wild birds and their habitats in Ireland, with a number of nature reserves, and part of BirdTrack. *www.birdwatchireland.ie*

BirdLife International A global collaboration of non-governmental organizations that works to conserve birds and their habitats. Its website holds a huge amount of information on species' range and status. *www.birdlife.org*

Flock Together A birdwatching organization for people of colour. *www.flocktogether.world*

Fatbirder Information about birdwatching worldwide. *www.fatbirder.com*

Eurobirding Information on birdwatching in Europe. *www.eurobirding.co.uk*

Xeno Canto A comprehensive collection of bird recordings. *www.xeno-canto.org*

Birdguides Information on identification and status. *www.birdguides.com*

BirdTrack A citizen science project to record names and numbers of birds seen. *www.bto.org/our-science/projects/birdtrack*

USEFUL READING

Here are some other DK books you might find interesting and helpful.

RSPB Pocket Birds of Britain and Europe

RSPB Pocket Garden Birdwatch

RSPB Birds of Britain and Europe: The Definitive Photographic Field Guide

How to Attract Birds to Your Garden

RSPB Complete Birds of Britain and Europe

RSPB What's that Bird?: The Simplest ID Guide Ever

Bird: The Definitive Visual Guide

USEFUL APPS

These are just some of the many apps available to help you identify the birds around you, via sound or image.

Merlin Bird ID	iBird Pro
BirdNET	eBird
ChirpOMatic	Seek
BirdID	iNaturalist

Index

Page numbers in **bold** refer to main entries

Acknowledgments

From the author

I would like to thank the fabulous team at DK for all their patient and painstaking work to make this book as perfect as possible. Stephanie Farrow has worked wonders with the editing, designers Ali Scrivens and Clare Joyce have made it accessible, clear and impressive, Rob Hume has drawn upon his enormous ornithological expertise and experience to produce a brilliant text, and Angeles Gavira and Michael Duffy have overseen the project with deft hands and enthusiasm. Thank you.

From the publisher

DK would like to thank Clare Joyce for design assistance, Salima Hirani for proofreading, and Helen Peters for the index.

92 **Alamy Stock Photo:** Arterra Picture Library / De Meester Johan. 93 **Getty Images / iStock:** CuorerouC (crb). **Getty Images:** Moment / Alan Tunnicliffe Photography (clb); Moment / Sandra Standbridge (cb). 94 **Alamy Stock Photo:** Arterra Picture Library / De Meester Johan (crb). **Dreamstime.com:** Anders93 (clb). 95 **Alamy Stock Photo:** Claude Balcaen / Biosphoto. 96-97 **Getty Images / iStock:** kvasay. 98 **Image Courtesy Flock Together:** Will Carr. 100 **Alamy Stock Photo:** AGAMI Photo Agency / Wil Leurs. 101 **Alamy Stock Photo:** Krys Bailey (cb). **Dreamstime.com:** Uschi Hering (clb); Wirestock (crb). 102 **Dorling Kindersley:** Chris Gomersall Photography (bl); Mike Lane (cl, cl/Blackbird, cr); Roger Tidman (crb, cb). **Dreamstime.com:** Borislav Borisov / Filev (cla); Isselee (cra). **Getty Images / iStock:** drakuliren (bc). 103 **Dorling Kindersley:** Mike Lane (tl); Roger Tidman (clb, bc). **Dreamstime.com:** Vasyl Helevachuk (cb); Wildlife World (cla, cla/Male Chaffinch, crb); Isselee (cra, cr). 104 **Getty Images:** Altaf Shah / 500px. 105 **Getty Images / iStock:** dan_chippendale (cb); Plougman (clb). **Getty Images:** Moment Open / Image by cuppyuppycake (clb). 106 **123RF.com:** Elena Duvernay (cra); Michael Lane (crb/Goldcrest). **Dorling Kindersley:** Roger Tidman (cl, cb). **Dreamstime.com:** Vasyl Helevachuk (cb); Wildlife World (crb/Blackcap). 107 **Dorling Kindersley:** Chris Gomersall Photography (tl); Melvin Grey (tc); Neil Fletcher (cl); E. J. Peiker (cb); Mike Lane (crb); Tim Loseby (clb); Roger Tidman (clb/Dove). **Dreamstime.com:** Keithpritchard (bc). 108 **Alamy Stock Photo:** blickwinkel / Koenig (clb). **Dorling Kindersley:** Chris Gomersall Photography (crb). **Getty Images:** Moment / Charmian Perkins (cb). 109 **Alamy Stock Photo:** Yorkshire Pics. 110 **123RF.com:** Juan Carlos Martnez Salvadores (cla). **Dorling Kindersley:** Chris Gomersall Photography; Tim Loseby (tl); Roger Wilmshurst (ca); Roger Tidman (crb, cr). **Dreamstime.com:** Gallinagomedia (cra); Keithpritchard (ca/Wagtail). **Getty Images / iStock:** drakuliren (cb). 111 **123RF.com:** Eric Isselee (bl). **Dorling Kindersley:** Chris Gomersall Photography (cl); Roger Wilmshurst (cla, bc). **Dreamstime.com:** Isselee (cra); Mikelane45 (crb). 112 **Dreamstime.com:** Grahammoore999 (cb). **Shutterstock.com:** Ken Griffiths (clb); Nigel Jarvis (crb). 113 **Alamy Stock Photo:** blickwinkel / P. Frischknecht. 114 **Dorling Kindersley:** Chris Gomersall Photography (tc, ca); Mike Lane (tr); Roger Wilmshurst (cb, br); E. J. Peiker (cb/Kittiwake). **Dreamstime.com:** Natursports (cr). **Fotolia:** Chrispo (bl). **Getty Images:** Michael Nolan (tl). 115 **Dorling Kindersley:** Chris Gomersall Photography (clb); Roger Wilmshurst (cra); Roger Tidman (cb). **Dreamstime.com:** Hakoar (br); Jeremy Richards (cla). **Getty Images / iStock:** Henk Bogaard (cb). 116 **Getty Images:** Moment / Vicki

Jauron, Babylon and Beyond Photography. 117 **Alamy Stock Photo:** dpa picture alliance (crb). **Dreamstime.com:** Menno67 (clb). **Shutterstock.com:** Pavlov Sergei888. 118 **Alamy Stock Photo:** imageBROKER.com GmbH & Co. KG / Thomas Hinsche (cl); Rob Read (tl). **Dorling Kindersley:** Mark Hamblin (cla, cr); Mike Lane (ca, cb); George McCarthy (cra); Roger Tidman (bc). 119 **Alamy Stock Photo:** blickwinkel / McPHOTO / NBT (crb); ephotocorp / Yogesh Bhandarkar (cb); Naturfoto-Online (crb/Eider). **Dorling Kindersley:** David Tipling, Windrush Photos (tl); Steve Young (tr, cra); Roger Tidman (ca); Mark Hamblin (cla); George McCarthy (clb); Mike Lane (cb/Plover). 120 **Alamy Stock Photo:** blickwinkel / AGAMI / R. Martin (clb). **Getty Images:** Moment / photography by Linda Lyon (cb). **Shutterstock.com:** Andi111 (crb). 121 **Alamy Stock Photo:** Hira Punjabi. 122 **Dorling Kindersley:** Mark Hamblin (cla/Pintail); Roger Tidman (cla, bl, bc); Windrush Photos / David Tipling (tc); Roger Wilmshurst; Mike Lane (clb, cb). 122-123 **Dreamstime.com:** Frank Fichtmueller (b). 123 **Dorling Kindersley:** Chris Gomersall (tl, cla); Mike Lane (tc, cr); Steve Young (tr, cb); George McCarthy (ca); Roger Tidman (cl, clb). 124 **Getty Images / iStock:** E+ / skynesher (crb). **Getty Images:** imageBROKER / Franz Christoph Robiller (clb); Moment / Sandra Standbridge (cb). 125 **Shutterstock.com:** Petr Simon. 126 **Dorling Kindersley:** Chris Gomersall Photography (cla); Roger Wilmshurst (tc); Mike Lane (tr, bl); George McCarthy (cra); David Cottridge (cr); Roger Tidman (br). **Dreamstime.com:** Ondej Prosick (cb). **Getty Images / iStock:** Film Studio Aves (tl). 127 **Dorling Kindersley:** Mark Hamblin (cla); Mike Lane (cra); Windrush Photos / David Tipling (crb); Roger Tidman (crb/Goosander). **Dreamstime.com:** Isselee (clb). 128-129 **Alamy Stock Photo:** Mint Images Limited (b). 129 **Alamy Stock Photo:** blickwinkel / W. Buchhorn / F. Hecker (tr); Klaus Steinkamp (tc). **Getty Images:** 500Px Plus / Claudio Cavalensi (tl). 130 **Dorling Kindersley:** Chris Gomersall Photography (tl); Mark Hamblin (tr, crb); David Tipling (cla); Roger Tidman (cra); E. J. Peiker (crb/Moorhen). **Dreamstime.com:** Rudmer Zwerver (clb). 131 **Dorling Kindersley:** Chris Gomersall Photography (c, bl); Roger Tidman (ca, br); Mike Lane (cra, clb, cb); Mark Hamblin (cr). 132-133 **Alamy Stock Photo:** RooM the Agency / kristianbell (b). 133 **Dreamstime.com:** Birdiegal717 (tr). **Getty Images / iStock:** Selim Kaya (tc). **Shutterstock.com:** LMIMAGES (tl). 134 **Depositphotos Inc:** kwasny222 (crb/Teal). **Dorling Kindersley:** Chris Gomersall Photography (ca, cla/Duck); Roger Wilmshurst (tc, cla/Female Shoveler, crb/Gadwall); Roger Tidman (tr, cra, cra/Goldeneye); Mike Lane (cla, cb, br); Chris Gomersall (clb). **Dreamstime.com:** Birdiegal717 (cl). **Shutterstock.com:** Alex Cooper Photography (crb).

135 **Dorling Kindersley:** Chris Gomersall Photography (bl); Mike Lane (ca); David Cottridge (cra); Steve Young (crb). **Dreamstime.com:** Miroslav Hlavko (cb); Isselee (br). 136 **Alamy Stock Photo:** FLPA. 137 **Dreamstime.com:** Irina Poleshikova (crb); Vladimir Soltys (clb). **Shutterstock.com:** Heliosphile (cb). 138 **Dorling Kindersley:** Chris Gomersall Photography (ca); Roger Tidman (cra, cb); Mike Lane (bl); Chris Gomersall (cb/Corn Bunting); David Tipling (crb). **Dreamstime.com:** Wildlife World (cl). 139 **Dorling Kindersley:** Chris Gomersall Photography (cb, br); George McCarthy (tl, tc); Chris Knights (tr); Mark Hamblin (ca); Roger Wilmshurst (cla); Mike Lane (cb/Gull, bl). **Dreamstime.com:** Daviesjk (cra); Mikelane45 (clb). 140 **Dreamstime.com:** Steve Byland (cb); Kostya Pazyuk (crb). **Getty Images / iStock:** Ian Newell (clb). 141 **Getty Images:** Lillian King. 142 **123RF.com:** Piotr Krzelak (crb). **Dorling Kindersley:** Mark Hamblin (cr, cb, ca); Roger Tidman (tl); Mikelane45 (tr); Windrush Photos / David Tipling (cla); Roger Wilmshurst (cra). **Dreamstime.com:** Henkbogaard (cl). **Getty Images / iStock:** Andyworks (tL). 143 **Dorling Kindersley:** Melvin Grey (crb); Roger Tidman (tl, tc); Steve Young (cra); Markus Varesvuo (cl); Mike Lane (clb, cb). **Dreamstime.com:** Vasyl Helevachuk (crb/siskin); Paul Reeves (ca); Wildlife World (clb/Flycatcher, bc). 144-145 **Alamy Stock Photo:** Nature Picture Library (b). 145 **Alamy Stock Photo:** wonderful-Earth.net (tc). **Dreamstime.com:** Mikelane45 (tl). **naturepl.com:** Alan Williams (tr). 146 **Dorling Kindersley:** Chris Gomersall Photography (clb/Whinchat); David Cottridge (tl); Steve Young (tc); Mike Lane (cra, clb); Roger Wilmshurst (c); Roger Tidman (cl); Mark Hamblin (bc). **Dreamstime.com:** Antonio Guillem (crb); Vasyl Helevachuk (ca); Martin Pelanek (crb/Saxicola). 147 **Dorling Kindersley:** David Cottridge (cl); Mark Hamblin (cra); Markus Varesvuo (c); Roger Tidman (cr); Mike Dunning (br). **Dreamstime.com:** Natalia Bubochkina (bc); Jarek2313 (cla). 148 **Alamy Stock Photo:** Andrew Parkinson (crb). **Shutterstock.com:** WildMedia (clb). 149 **Alamy Stock Photo:** imageBROKER / Bernd Zoller. 150 **Alamy Stock Photo:** Wildscotphotos (br). **Dorling Kindersley:** Chris Gomersall Photography (crb); Philip Newman (clb); Hanne Eriksen / Jens Eriksen (clb); Mike Lane (cr); Windrush Photos / David Tipling (cra). **Dreamstime.com:** Agami Photo Agency (crb/Ouzel); Outdoorsman. **Getty Images / iStock:** Marc Guyt (tc). 151 **Dorling Kindersley:** Chris Gomersall Photography (bc); Roger Tidman (tl); Mark Hamblin (cl); Mike Lane (cr, cb, crb); David Cottridge (bl); Chris Gomersall (crb/Ptarmigan). **Getty Images / iStock:** JMrocek (tr).

All other images © Dorling Kindersley

160 ACKNOWLEDGMENTS